ADVANCE PRAISE FOR *PART-TIME IS PLENTY*

"If you are depressed about the state of the church and you want to stay that way, do not read this book. You will find no commiserating or complaining here. And if you want to turn back the clock and protect the church's past from the future, these words are not for you. But if you are ready to change your mind and be constructively challenged, read on. This book is filled with true stories of excellence and creativity that will inspire you. What I love most about this book is that the author is unapologetically excited about the new thing God is doing in the church right now. A part-time pastor himself, and a respected journalist, Jeffrey MacDonald was clearly called to write this book for just such a time as this."

—**Lillian Daniel**, preacher, teacher, and author of
Tired of Apologizing for a Church I Don't Belong To

"Increasing numbers of mainline Protestant clergy are becoming part-time pastors. Jeffrey McDonald reframes this phenomenon as more than a financial necessity; it's a God-given opportunity. Whereas many congregations think of a part-time pastor as a sign of scarcity, McDonald reminds us that the American church's time of greatest vitality was led by part-time pastors. He gives practical advice for how pastors can move from bein source of pastoral care and leadership into the role of th team leader, uncovering and developing the God-giv of the laity and leading their churches in a way that de the laity of their baptismal responsibility to be Christ in this time and place. This is a hopeful, helpful book f time as this."

—**Will Willimon**, United Methodist bishop; Profess
Practice of Christian Ministry, Duke Divinity Sch
author of *Leading with the Sermon: Preaching as Lea*

"Jeffrey MacDonald has written a parable in this book: taking assumptions about the church—and full-time clergy serving in it—and inviting the reader to reconsider what we think we know. MacDonald challenges the idea that part-time clergy service is bad news for congregations and the ordained ministers who serve them and offers examples and insights that clearly show the opposite. Part-time ministry is an opportunity for creativity and focusing on what matters most: sharing the love of God with the world. This is a very timely and extremely important look at how we are reimagining ministry across the church, and it is good news for those of us looking for signs of church renewal and revitalization."

—**Catherine Caimano**, Free Range Priest

"*Part-Time Is Plenty* can help the church today reclaim a truth our ancestors knew well: the church is not defined by whether or not it has a full-time pastor. Jeffrey MacDonald's conviction that a renewal of lay leadership in the church can energize congregations takes us back to our roots and forward into the new thing that God is doing among us today. I believe this book will help many in the church to dream new dreams and see new visions."

—**Joan Gray**, Presbyterian pastor and author of *Sailboat Church*

"I read this book with great interest as a judicatory leader but also as someone who had a season of part-time ministry myself. Helpful and informative, with ideas to spark the imagination and stretch the soul of any reader from the person in the pew to the pastor to the judicatory or seminary, this book is one to highly recommend as we encounter, lead, and engage ministry in this fast-changing landscape for congregations and communities. This is a conversation that needs to continue beyond the pages of this book. There are more avenues to explore and more opportunities in our future than we presently imagine to get on board with what the Spirit is doing with the church."

—**Shannan Vance-Ocampo**, general presbyter, Presbytery of Southern New England

PART-TIME IS PLENTY

PART-TIME IS PLENTY

*Thriving without
Full-Time Clergy*

G. JEFFREY MacDONALD

WESTMINSTER
JOHN KNOX PRESS
LOUISVILLE • KENTUCKY

First edition
Published by Westminster John Knox Press
Louisville, Kentucky

20 21 22 23 24 25 26 27 28 29—10 9 8 7 6 5 4 3 2 1

Unless otherwise indicated, Scripture quotations are from the New Revised Standard Version of the Bible, copyright © 1989 by the Division of Christian Education of the National Council of the Churches of Christ in the U.S.A., and are used by permission.

Book design by Drew Stevens
Cover design by designpointinc.com

Library of Congress Cataloging-in-Publication Data

Names: MacDonald, G. Jeffrey, author.
Title: Part-time is plenty : thriving without full-time clergy / G. Jeffrey
    MacDonald.
Description: First edition. | Louisville : Westminster John Knox Press,
    2020. | Includes bibliographical references. | Summary: "Churches
    experiencing numerical and financial decline may dread the day when they
    can no longer afford a full-time pastor. Freeing up funds that would go
    to a full-time salary sure would help the budget-maybe even enough to
    turn things around-but is it even possible to run effective ministries
    with just a half- or quarter-time professional? Journalist and part-time
    pastor Jeffrey MacDonald says yes-churches can grow more vibrant than
    ever, tapping into latent energy and undiscovered gifts, revitalizing
    worship, and engaging in more effective ministry with the community.
    Readers get a much-needed playbook for helping congregations to thrive
    with a part-time ministry model. They learn to see the model in a new
    light: to stop viewing part-time as a problem to be eradicated and to
    instead embrace it as a divine gift that facilitates a higher level of
    lay engagement, responsibility, playfulness, and creativity"-- Provided
    by publisher.
Identifiers: LCCN 2020001722 (print) | LCCN 2020001723 (ebook) | ISBN
    9780664265991 (paperback) | ISBN 9781611649932 (ebook)
Subjects: LCSH: Clergy, Part-time. | Lay ministry. | Church management. |
    Pastoral theology.
Classification: LCC BV676.5 .M33 2020 (print) | LCC BV676.5 (ebook) | DDC
    253--dc23
LC record available at https://lccn.loc.gov/2020001722
LC ebook record available at https://lccn.loc.gov/2020001723

Most Westminster John Knox Press books are available at special quantity discounts when purchased in bulk by corporations, organizations, and special-interest groups. For more information, please e-mail SpecialSales@wjkbooks.com.

To my mother, Lois MacDonald,
who taught me to recognize God's voice and fingerprints
in unexpected places.
And to my late father, George L. MacDonald Jr.,
who always believed in me.

CONTENTS

ACKNOWLEDGMENTS

Part-time is plenty . . . as long as others step up too. Without their gifts and passions, an ordained pastor can't get far alone. The same holds true for the work for book-writing, especially when it's done alongside other jobs that don't slow down for authors. I couldn't have written this book without sustained support and forbearance from many people who, like me, believed it worthy of some sacrifice.

I needed others to believe with me that if a few congregations are thriving with part-time clergy, then we could likely find others and disseminate their surprising, instructive, and inspiring stories. I found such partners at the BTS Center, a Maine-based nonprofit that awarded me a grant to visit congregations in ten states and report on their experiences. Bob Grove-Markwood was instrumental in opening this door and providing a variety of venues for me to share emergent findings and absorb much-needed feedback. Pamela Shellberg devoted many hours to thinking deeply about this project, asking essential questions, and sharing concepts that gave me mental scaffolding to climb. Alyssa Lodewick was patient, inquisitive, and confident that we were onto something important as a team and would see it through to completion together. I could not have asked for better partners than these BTS Center staffers and the board of directors, which took an active interest in my research. Working in close conjunction with them, the United Church of Christ's Maine Conference Minister Debora Blood believed in the importance of this work from the beginning. She added to it as an encourager, thought partner and invaluable field guide to the Maine religious landscape.

I also needed cooperative congregations who would allow a nosy reporter to visit and then hang around for hours interviewing everyone he could find. I found twenty such congregations, as well as others who took my calls and answered countless questions. Each of the churches mentioned in these pages was graciously open and patient with me; I am truly thankful for their trust. Because I visited so many, not all are mentioned in the book, but all nonetheless shaped my understanding and vision. Hospitable hosts who don't get as much ink yet deserve a shout of gratitude include the Rev. Susie Maxwell of Centre Street Congregational in Machias, Maine; the Rev. Dorothy Gremillion of Grace Episcopal in Llano, Texas; the Rev. Sacia Vik of Lake City Christian in Seattle, Washington; the Rev. Tom Bentley of Trinity Congregational in Gloucester, Massachusetts; the Rev. Catherine Gregg of the Episcopal Diocese of Nevada and the Rev. Christie Leavitt of St. Matthew's Episcopal in Las Vegas, Nevada.

Editors at various publications helped me turn raw research into initial reports. At *The Living Church*, John Schussler, Doug LeBlanc, and Christopher Wells let me publish a deep-dive series on vital congregations with part-time clergy. They also kept my correspondent load mercifully light in the summer of 2019 while I finished the manuscript. Scott Armstrong at the *Christian Science Monitor* provided space and thoughtful editing for my cover story in the weekly magazine. Sally Hicks at *Faith*

& Leadership further shepherded my thinking on this topic with probing questions and feedback as my early thoughts on part-time ministry models made their way onto faithandleadership.com with support from Duke Divinity School and the Lilly Foundation.

Finding a home for this book was a smooth journey thanks to several generous souls. My author friend and fellow UCC pastor Lillian Daniel provided a supportive ear and encouraging thoughts. Her agent, Greg Daniel, drew on experience in guiding me to query Westminster John Knox Press. At WJK Press, I found a most patient and wise partner in Acquisitions Editor Jessica Miller Kelley. Her feedback on my proposal moved the concept in a tighter, more fruitful direction, and her insightful edits found all the weak spots (I hope) before going to press. I am grateful to everyone in editorial, production, marketing, and other departments at WJK Press for helping bring this project to fruition and for making the book as accessible as possible.

Along the way, my congregation at First Parish Church of Newbury has been incredibly supportive. My flock kindly let me reduce my workload by 50 percent for six months so that I could be absent on Sundays (read: let me be in worship elsewhere with my notebook out) during the research phase. When time came to finish the manuscript, the congregation gave me a wide berth as I holed up in air-conditioned spaces for a few hot months to get it done. I am constantly grateful to this faithful group for simply walking with me on this part-time ministry journey. We challenge each other for the better. We're discovering together how to make disciples within what is for Newbury a new ministry model. What a blessing to be in this together.

Friends have been indispensable during this time, especially when my father, Dr. George L. MacDonald Jr., passed away in March 2019. I worked through ideas for the book over late-night calls and walks in the woods with Eric Wybenga; in a canoe on East Coast rivers with Frederick Simmons; over diner breakfasts with the Rev. Ross Varney; atop the Atlantic Ocean's wind and waves in my sailboat, the Bonnie Lass, with the likes of Richard Coleman, Andrew Boylan, and Ryan McDonnell. Ideas always need lots of refining before they're ready for prime time. These good folks among others too numerous to list have helped me winnow what now seems worthy to publish. I give thanks to God for their wisdom and friendship.

Family members have been wonderful as well. My late father's boundless interest in every project I ever took up and his confidence that I could and should pursue this one, my second book, gives buoyancy to all my work. My sister, Bonnie, has been a thoughtful sounding board and gracious hostess when the topic of part-time ministry has arisen at holiday gatherings. My nieces, Olivia and Louisa Gould, have brought incisive questions and steady encouragement. The boys in my life, Robert and Ryan Hayes have been good friends and steadfast allies in every type of season, and we've had many together. Their mother, Debora Hayes, has been with me through life's troughs and peaks for a long time. She has endured hearing the work-in-progress details of countless projects that have become my obsessions over the years. Her patient listening and thoughtful input shaped this book for the better. My mother, Lois MacDonald, has never wavered in her loving support. Her faith in Jesus Christ and her commitment to his church are never-ending sources of inspiration.

As a writer with a strong sense of calling, I believe everything I write has a final form that it's supposed to take. I sometimes struggle mightily to find it, while other times it flows fairly smoothly into its appointed vessel. Somehow God always provides the necessary process and grace. For this truth and for all the people who've had a hand in making it so this time around, I give thanks.

G. Jeffrey MacDonald
Swampscott, Mass.
Nov. 5, 2019

INTRODUCTION

From the outside, First Parish Church (United Church of Christ) in Newbury, Massachusetts, appeared to be chugging along reasonably well after 377 years of ministry. A small group of faithful souls still gathered every Sunday morning. A preschool met in the downstairs hall on weekdays. More than forty area residents tended organic gardens out back in what had become a model project of land recovery and stewardship. Sure, the building needed a paint job, but that seemed minor . . . except that it was symptomatic of a larger problem that was fueling conflict and rapidly imperiling the church's survival.

First Parish was hemorrhaging money for one main reason: it couldn't afford its full-time pastor. Clergy compensation (salary, housing allowance, and benefits) was costing the church nearly six figures a year, yet weekly offerings totaled only a fraction of what was needed. So great was the discrepancy that, together with some hefty building expenses, the weight of full-time compensation hastened the depletion of a $575,000 endowment fund in less than four years. Finally, as Christmas approached in 2012, there was nothing left to spend. Bills were piling up. The pastor quit suddenly. Despondent parishioners prepared to disband. I received a call in my capacity as a supply preacher. Was I available to lead a few final worship services? Saddened to hear this historic church was so near its end, I agreed to help out however I could.

I'd been there a few weeks when the congregation changed its mind and decided to continue in ministry—albeit with a radically different ministry model. The pastorate would be slashed from forty hours to ten hours a week. The church administrator position would be eliminated entirely. Because I have a full-time job as a writer, I was financially able to consider this part-time call when the church offered it to me. But parishioners and I harbored many of the same questions: How could the church possibly do effective, impactful ministry without a full-time pastor? Who would organize programs, lead adult education groups, represent the church at community events, visit the sick at home and in the hospital, and perform many other ministry tasks?

None of us had any idea how this would happen, especially in a church that had long relied on a full-time pastor to do all those things and more. But the church's only choice, it seemed, was either to try a part-time model or close down a ministry begun in 1635. With more than a little hope and prayer, we decided to try.

It gives me joy to report that eight years later, First Parish is thriving by several measures in Newbury, and I'm still in the pulpit part-time. Finances are stable with budgets balanced (mostly) and a gift that helped restart an endowment fund. Thanks to many dedicated volunteers, our four-year-old food pantry feeds upward of 150 people a week. But I'm no rescue hero or turnaround guru with a tale of personal prowess to tell. On the contrary, I've been learning from other congregations what I wish I'd known—and what all of us wish First Parish had known before I arrived. Congregations *can* experience *more* vitality, not less, after switching to part-time clergy. They can get there by following a few tested steps and principles, no matter where they're located or what denomination they belong to. How I wish we'd had their insights when we embarked on this journey in 2012.

But they were hidden. I know because I looked online, in bookstores, and in libraries. What was written about part-time ministry was largely focused on the pastor in the vein of encouragement for labor in the vineyard, for instance, or tips for how to juggle two jobs plus a family. What we needed was a primer on how *laypeople* can be sustained and impactful while the pastor is off earning a secular paycheck forty or more hours a week. That book didn't turn up in any searches, though hopefully now it will.

Toni Morrison reportedly said: "If you find a book you really want to read but it hasn't been written yet, then you must write it."[1] Heeding her advice, I'm adding a layer: this is the book I not only wanted to read but one I desperately *needed* to read. Like more and more of my part-time clergy peers, I'm not the type of part-time pastor who's semiretired from ministry, needing something to do or longing to feel loved by an adoring congregation. Monday through Friday, I'm reporting on deadline for the likes of *The Boston Globe* and the *Christian Science Monitor*, covering subjects from trends in religious life to federal murder trials. Sometimes I'm on assignment 1,500 or 2,000 miles away from my church. The only way my congregation is going to be effective is if we leverage together the many talents in the pews and get creatively missional alongside partners in the community. But how does this happen when parishioners haven't been theologically trained and the pastor isn't available even to coach the lay leaders? Where does a church begin when it's been used to relying on a professional to do all the theological and ministerial "heavy lifting"? Isn't this a bit like hoping a new homeowner will quickly learn how to repair sinks, pipes, and toilets without even as much as a tutorial in plumbing?

I knew I wasn't alone in asking these questions. Tens of thousands of mainline Protestant congregations have unwittingly done away with full-time clergy in recent decades because they can no longer afford the luxury of retaining a cleric who's assigned solely to one flock. Many have arrived at this situation much as First Parish did: abruptly, with little or no planning, and with no game plan for powerfully impacting the communities beyond their walls. These churches simply fell into it after trying, as First Parish did, to hold on to their full-time pastorates for as long as possible. If anyone needs a primer and fast, it's all of us— laypeople, pastors, denominational staffers, friends, and supportive neighbors of local churches—who've suddenly found ourselves taking a test we haven't studied for. And for those thousands of mainline congregations considering a shift to part-time when their baby boomer pastors retire or when their budgets can no longer justify a full-time salary, a primer on how congregations have done it well could be helpful too.

SEEKING CLUES IN CAMOUFLAGE

I decided in 2016 to stop wondering and go find some answers. I proposed a research project to dig into the lives of congregations that have done what's commonly thought to be impossible: they've attained more vitality after reinventing (or rediscovering) themselves without full-time clergy. Vitality would be defined tightly enough to be meaningful but also broadly enough to allow for variation across contexts.

I adapted marks of vitality from a report put out by the United Church of Christ[2] and framed criteria that bring telling stories to the surface. Every congregation would need to have gone from being financially unsustainable (i.e., chronically spending beyond its means) to financially stable (keeping spending in line with income). All in the sample could now balance their budgets in a sustainable, principled way. Beyond that, each would bear at least one additional mark of vitality such as growing worship attendance, increasing members' engagement in ministries, expanding mission outreach into the community, growing the budget via disciplined stewardship practices or increasing mission giving. The BTS Center in Portland, Maine, awarded me a $20,000 grant to delve into congregations that fit the bill and then publish my findings with hopes that many congregations could learn from the vital ones' experiences.

At first, I expected to find six or eight case studies—enough to prove the species exists and run a few tests. But the research bore more fruit than anyone expected. In ten states from New England and the Mid-Atlantic to the Southwest and Pacific Northwest, I visited twenty vital, thriving mainline Protestant congregations with part-time clergy. I gathered information about a few others by telephone and email. The instructive, inspiring experiences of these congregations provide the basis for this book.

At first, I wondered if I'd be able to pull it off. When I queried middle judicatory officials for vital congregations with part-time clergy, I heard a common refrain: "We don't have any." "Not any?" I asked, bewildered. None, they explained, because if they were truly vital, they wouldn't have part-time clergy. They'd be able to afford full-time clergy, as all healthy congregations presumably can do.

After a few calls like this, I realized I wasn't facing a dearth of empirical data but rather a habitual way of thinking that simply equated healthy with having full-time clergy. I was convinced that even though some, perhaps most, congregations experienced decline after switching to part-time clergy, others surely did not. I'd known congregations that had long managed with part-time clergy; some must have transitioned from full-timers and come to thrive on the other side. It turned out my instincts were right: dozens have done just that. But there are reasons why their stories are so hard to find. First and foremost, they aren't looking to be found. And their full-time peers aren't eager to bring them to light either.

Like a camouflaged species that blends invisibly into the landscape, these congregations are hidden in plain sight. They're churches we've all passed a thousand times on the way to the grocery store but never stopped to go inside. Nothing in their public presentation says, "our pastor works part-time." On websites and at their physical locations, they look like churches with full-time pastors insofar as they meet weekly, host support groups, gather committees, and so forth. They do their best to keep their buildings up by spending money that's no longer needed to pay full-time salaries anymore. As maintainers of appearances, they do quite well. That's not an accident.

They don't self-identify as having part-time clergy because they don't want to call attention to the fact. They've imbibed the stigma about part-time clergy and their congregations. That stigma wrongly suggests they have less to offer to individuals and families in search of spiritual community. They're often ashamed and apologetic about having part-time clergy. Some hasten to insist it's only a temporary situation until they can get caught up financially, hire a full-timer, and be a "real" church again. The ones who know who's part-time and who's not in a given region are middle judicatory officials, but they're often predisposed not to see vitality in the absence of a full-time pastor. Such dynamics reinforce the low self-esteem that's common among congregations with part-time clergy. Even those with inspiring, instructive stories of vitality have routinely convinced themselves nobody would want to hear from them. After all, they sheepishly say, we're not proud of the fact that we can't afford a full-time pastor. Who would be?

But all this hiding in plain sight runs enormous risks for the future of congregations and the positive impacts they've had for generations. Quietly mystified about how to adapt and thrive after full-time clergy, congregations that have made the switch unfortunately can and often do continue to decline. Unable to find each other, they don't learn from one another's success stories and emerging best practices. They try to project a public face that implies a conventional clergy staffing level but belies the truth: this is a different breed of congregation. In its difference, this breed offers opportunities that one would be hard-pressed to find in a church with full-time clergy. Raising awareness that these churches exist, have unique blessings to offer, and are capable of thriving more than before marks an essential first step toward their brightening future.

A SPRING BREAKS FORTH IN THE DESERT

With some digging, I found churches thriving after full-time clergy and warming to the idea of sharing their stories. In southwest Washington state, where a strong entrepreneurial culture influences even the mainline church world, a regional director for the Evangelical Lutheran Church in America quickly grasped what I was seeking. She pointed me to three congregations that perfectly fit the bill. In Nevada, I found Episcopal congregations that have recently worked out the kinks and ramped up missions despite adversity because that's what happens in Nevada, where most Episcopal congregations can't afford even one full-timer. In Virginia, Presbyterians weren't used to thinking about role model congregations with part-time clergy, but one call led to another. Eventually, a field guide emerged who could point me to an Arlington church that was vital in multiple ways. That congregation, Clarendon Presbyterian Church, had saved its pastor from burnout by cutting back to part-time a few years earlier. Bingo, I thought. Congregations are indeed finding new life after full-time clergy. Let's keep their stories coming and learn all we can from them.

Once I got the knack for ferreting out these diamonds in the rough, I realized I had more than a handful of interesting case studies. A sample of ten grew to twenty, and that was still just a slice of the landscape. I assembled a diverse cross section including rural, suburban, urban, liberal, conservative, predominantly straight, substantially gay, and inclusive of all the largest mainline Protestant denominations. Racial diversity was harder to find because of what I'd set out to learn. I wanted to know how congregations attain more vitality after switching from full-time to part-time clergy, and it turns out that phenomenon is primarily found among white-majority congregations. To be sure, ethnic and racial minority congregations have extensive experience finding vitality under part-time pastorates, which have been normative in many African American and new immigrant contexts. However, because these churches never had full-time clergy to begin with, they haven't made the transition from full- to part-time clergy, which was the focus of my research. Though I would have liked to see more skin color diversity in my sample, I found that predominantly white congregations are distinctly experiencing challenges associated with diminishing affluence, clergy cutbacks, and quests for new vitality in the midst of all the change. As we'll see, their paths to success include turning outward and forging partnerships, sometimes with more diverse congregations and other types of groups.

As I visited these churches and wore parishioners' patience thin with all my questions, I began to notice surprising themes. I found, for instance, that vital congregations are shedding conventional wisdom about who's supposed to do what in a congregation. They part ways with a pack that tends to assume rigidly fixed roles for clergy and laity. Conversely, a congregation won't thrive if it assumes, despite what's permitted within their respective denominational polities, that only clergy can do a host of duties and then slashes clergy hours to save money. Yet such predictable decline is exactly what happens in scores of congregations that go part-time and then won't reconsider who can and should do what in light of diminished resources.

Many times in this quest, I heard denominational staffers argue that it's not possible to come up with a playbook for congregations with part-time clergy because every local situation is different. With all due respect, that's a cop-out. Local variation in approach is of course necessary, but congregations can follow a system that helps more than their denominations realize. They can ask particular questions to identify their unique gifts, assets, and mission. They can design pastorates that aren't beholden to prior models used in their congregations, but instead reflect a pastor's gifts and a community's needs. They can develop latent potential within the ranks of laity. They can forge strategic partnerships. They can advocate for renewed relationships with brothers and sisters in Christ, who are in positions to help build them up and help them flourish as precious members of the one body. Such steps can be adapted to any local context. Readers will find in pages ahead many tips for doing just that.

First, however, a few words about definitions and terms. "Congregations with part-time clergy" is a terribly awkward and wordy phrase, but it appears often in these pages because it is sufficiently descriptive (and because the Christian world hasn't yet come up with a better term). Chapter 4 searches for a more effective moniker, but as that quest continues, I use "part-time congregations" at times as shorthand. I do this with some regret because they are 100 percent congregations; they exist as church for each other and for the world 100 percent of the time. But for the purposes of this book, it refers to congregations that have no full-time clergy serving in their local settings. It implies nothing beyond that.

Congregations with part-time clergy are defined as those that have a pastor serving in their local setting fewer than thirty-five hours per week. A church might have a clergyperson who works full-time as clergy but divides that time between two local churches. Both of those churches fit my definition of congregations with part-time clergy. In that scenario, each would be counted separately as a church with part-time clergy, even though they have a pastor who regards clergy as his or her full-time work. Other congregations have so-called bivocational clergy who aren't called solely to ministry but also work in another field or as a homemaker. Still others have an officially retired clergyperson who serves on a part-time basis. Hence this is a book about congregations, not about clergy per se and not solely about congregations with bivocational clergy. It's about congregations whose clergy serve part-time in those local church settings. Clunky, yes, but important to define.

These congregations are mainline Protestant. That means they're affiliated with denominations that trace their roots in America to the colonial era and allow room for liberal as well as conservative Christian theologies. My sample doesn't represent all such denominations but does include congregations affiliated with the some of the largest ones: the United Methodist Church, the Evangelical Lutheran Church in America, the Episcopal Church, the Presbyterian Church (U.S.A.), the United Church of Christ and the Christian Church (Disciples of Christ). Though they come from various denominations, their experiences bear many similarities and can be instructive across denominational lines. Descriptions of what the congregations are doing generally refer, unless otherwise noted, to what I witnessed in late 2016 and 2017 when I visited and conducted interviews.

WHAT'S AHEAD:
UNLEASHING THE POWER TO THRIVE

Chapter 1 confronts the challenging reality. Tens of thousands of mainline congregations now rely solely on part-time pastors for their clerical leadership. How to help them thrive has become a vexing question. Much in our denominational cultures is sabotaging the potentially bright prospects of congregations with part-time clergy. Yet some are quietly proving that a better, more vital way is within reach for those willing to organize themselves a bit differently.

Chapter 2 ushers in the most crucial players: laypeople in congregations. It explores what laity do differently in congregations that saw vitality increase after they went part-time. It offers tips for what to do before, during, and after the establishment of new roles for laypeople. Readers get a sense for denominational variations and how to thrive by adapting in their respective contexts.

Chapter 3 looks at clergy, who play essential, albeit revamped roles in these congregations. It considers three models: pastor as equipper, as ambassador, and as one of several specialized, part-time staffers. It delves into keys to success and offers tips for making the necessary mental and emotional shifts. Denominational differences are considered as clergy learn to embrace more, not less, of their respective traditions.

Chapter 4 explores the role of judicatory officials and denominational cultures. Judicatories, sometimes unknowingly or unwittingly, often bring unhelpful assumptions about congregations with part-time clergy. This chapter provides reasons and tips for undoing those assumptions and embracing a more productive way, as modeled in specific examples from my research.

Chapter 5 deals with theological education for both the part-time pastor and the laity, who will need it more than they have in the past. It confronts how the shift to part-time clergy has major implications and fallout for the way we train (or don't train). It lifts up promising examples that are gaining traction on the education landscape. It also calls for modified expectations around training and an evolving infrastructure to support it.

Chapter 6 considers how vitality is enhanced in these congregations via partnerships that transcend traditional siloed thinking and engage the wider religious and secular worlds. Teaming up to share missional capacities as well as building space and administrative support is bearing fruit. Partnering has even more potential as we think about who in surrounding communities is yearning for the types of opportunities uniquely afforded by congregations with part-time clergy.

It's time for vital congregations with part-time clergy to come out of the shadows, shake off their shame, and be recognized as distinctive contributors to God's feast— much like those who got a late invitation in the parable of the Wedding Banquet (Luke 14:7–14). They have a renewing role to play in a season marked by tighter budgets and creative repurposing of assets for holy purposes. Yet they've ironically been cast aside, barely noticed in an American culture that often celebrates only what is big or growing at a breakneck clip.

Perhaps we're ready to see the church of the future and get a running start toward that end in the pages to follow.

Chapter 1

GOODBYE TO BIAS, STIGMA, AND IDOLS

*Recovering Ministry as It's Been
Done through the Ages*

The Episcopal Church is well-known for grand stone cathedrals, pageantry in ritual, and distinguished members. But a much humbler and seldom-discussed reality defines day-to-day life for 46 percent of Episcopal congregations. More than 2,900 Episcopal congregations have no full-time paid clergy. Thirteen percent of domestic Episcopal congregations rely on unpaid priests or lay leaders, while the other 33 percent pay a priest to work part-time in that setting.[1] These congregations are hiding in plain sight. From the roadside, they look like others where the full-time priest is always available in emergencies, on hand to meet contractors, and ready on weekdays to lead a mid-morning Bible study, or counsel a distraught parishioner.

But these churches are decidedly different in a way that's seldom acknowledged in public. Between Sunday Eucharists, these clergy are off doing other things during the week: working other jobs, for instance, or staying home with young kids. Their congregations can't afford to keep them on the payroll full-time, which represents a giant adjustment for many. In many cases, congregants had gotten used to having clergy take care of myriad tasks, ranging from troubleshooting conflict situations to representing the church around town. These churches now aim to experience vitality while no longer relying on clergy to spearhead all the programs and always be the "professional Christian" in the group, ready with a smooth prayer or dollop of spiritual wisdom for any occasion. If they haven't already found vitality after full-time clergy, they need to learn how it happens.

According to diocesan staffers, however, the majority of these churches don't know how to be vital without a full-time shepherd to lead them. They're in a state of plateau or decline. They don't have the wherewithal to evangelize, be visible around town, or offer the type of programming that attracts newcomers and keeps them coming back. Such perennial challenges have been decades in the making in the Episcopal Diocese of Western Massachusetts, where about 50 percent of congregations rely on part-time clergy. Yet even the diocesan staffer responsible for cultivating health in local churches is still searching for a winning formula. A couple of years ago, she asked part-time clergy and lay leaders from three Pioneer Valley congregations to tell her what's the biggest gift and what's the biggest challenge of a reduced-pastorate model. They all answered that the greatest gift and challenge are the same thing: laypeople stepping up into leadership.

"It's the challenge because there are things you didn't realize the clergyperson did," said Pamela Mott, Canon to the Ordinary in the Episcopal Diocese of Western Massachusetts. "Contacting the oil company, running off the bulletins, handling pastoral care, community outreach, and community connections. That doesn't have to be the clergyperson who does all that. . . . But it's a challenge because the clergyperson has done it for so long in our congregations."

Shifting to part-time can touch off a wave of emotions that congregations aren't expecting or feeling prepared to handle. The prospect of taking up portions of the sprawling ministry mantle left behind by the last full-time cleric can seem daunting or overwhelming. I've witnessed worry coloring eyes and straining voices of stalwart church members as they speculate about what it means for their proud, historic church to be taking what feels like a humbling, unwanted step into part-time ministry. All of us want reassurance that God has not forsaken the divine plantings in our local soil. Just as much, we yearn to know that in going part-time we have not failed those—our congregants and communities, ancestors and descendants, or our Maker—whom we often perceive to be counting on faithfulness to come from us. These ruminations can be overdone and forgetful of the grace and providence that surround our days. Yet we still find ourselves awakening to the fact that much is at stake, and we want to get it right.

Learning how to thrive after switching to part-time clergy does not have to be a confounding puzzle either for the Episcopal Church or for other mainline Protestant denominations where part-time is increasingly the norm. Congregations can and do find vitality after full-time clergy. They're churches like St. John's Lutheran Church in Lakewood, Washington, where worship attendance doubled from twenty-five to fifty in the five years after it went part-time. Over the same time, mission giving at St. John's jumped from zero to 7 percent of the budget. Up the road in Kent, Washington, St. Columba's Episcopal Church saw attendance leap 44 percent (from fifty-five to seventy-nine) in the three years after the pastorate went part-time. At Christ Episcopal Church in Bethel, Vermont, mission giving jumped as funds formerly marked for clergy salary were redeployed in part to help neighbors in need. In

Maine, children's ministries took off at Tuttle Road United
Methodist Church in Cumberland and also at New Sharon
Congregational Church (United Church of Christ) in
New Sharon as the more flexible leadership led to church-
wide experimentation that bore new fruit in unexpected,
jubilantly received ways.

These congregations, among others, are letting go
of assumptions about clergy roles and renegotiating who
does what in the church. Laypeople are getting an overdue
chance to spread their wings and flourish in ministry
when clergy are no longer at the center of it all. How these
congregations deliver on the promise of part-time ministry
varies depending on lots of factors, including context
and faith tradition. Across the board, however, inspiring
examples show it can be done. If these congregations
can do it, others can too, even if they've made mistakes
or misjudged circumstances in the past. Those best-
positioned to succeed are getting a leg up by removing
mental roadblocks and acting early enough to start sharing
leadership in a fresh way. First, they need to understand
why congregations so often struggle after going part-time
and what needs to be done differently to get better results.
That involves getting a handle on what's driving the trend
and the extent to which congregations have options in how
they respond.

SMALLER BUDGETS CALL FOR
BIGGER DECISIONS

Mainline congregations aren't waiting for their denominations to figure out a recipe for being vital with part-time
clergy at the helm. At least 26,000 have already gone part-

time.[2] About 43 percent of U.S. mainline congregations have no full-time paid clergy, according to preliminary data from the 2018–19 National Congregations Study.[3] Other research suggests strong momentum toward part-time pastorates. A national survey from the Hartford Institute for Religion Research found that in 2015, 38 percent of American churches had part-time clergy. That marked a dramatic increase from 29 percent just five years earlier.[4] We'll need more data before we know how far the part-time trajectory has gone, but the upward trend has thus far shown no signs of leveling off.

The part-time trend is noticeable by region, which is the level at which denominations keep most of their data on part-time congregations. That is, if they track the phenomenon at all. Snapshots from 2016 shed some light. Seventy percent of New England's United Methodist congregations had no full-time clergy in their local settings. That was up from 55 percent five years earlier. In Maine, 68 percent of United Church of Christ congregations were relying on part-time clergy. In the Episcopal Diocese of Northern Michigan, none of the twenty-four congregations had a full-time priest. In Vermont, Northern California, and Nevada, the majority of Episcopal congregations relied solely on part-time clergy then, just as they do today.

What used to be a phenomenon of rural America is now increasingly an urban and suburban one as well. One 2019 study finds the percentage of clergy working second jobs is growing in America's less religious regions and those with high costs of living, notably in the largely urban and suburban Northeast.[5] Example: in the Episcopal Diocese of Pittsburgh, three-quarters of congregations have no full-time clergy. What's more, the percentage of U.S. clergy employed fewer than thirty-five hours a week has

gradually and steadily doubled from eight percent in 1976
to 16 percent in 2018 (see figure 1). Faith communities that
once seemed immune to economic pressures are, even in a
strong economy, finding they must adjust to new realities
exacerbated by worship attendance trends. And that means
rediscovering what seems counterintuitive in America but
makes perfect sense according to the Bible: an underdog
people can triumph over adversity, even when belts tighten
and material supports fade away. That's when the faithful
lean all the more on one another and rely on the Holy Spirit
in a whole new way.

The main cause driving the part-time trend is simple:
money. Americans aren't going to church like they used

FIGURE 1.

TRENDS IN PART-TIME (<35 HOURS/WEEK) CLERGY

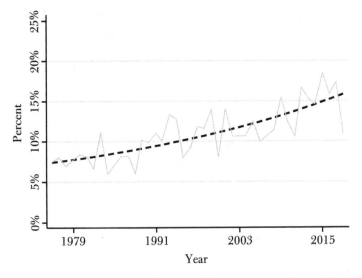

Source: Cyrus Schleifer, PhD, analysis of U.S. Bureau of Labor Statistics data, looking at individuals
who identify clergy as their primary occupation (this includes various denominations, not just mainline Protestants). Sample includes about 8,000 clergy over forty-two years. Used with permission
from Dr. Cyrus Schleifer, University of Oklahoma. All rights reserved by Dr. Schleifer.

to. In 2007, 54 percent of Americans attended religious services at least monthly. By 2019, only 45 percent did.[6] Meanwhile from 2005 to 2015, congregations saw their average Sunday attendance drop 38 percent from 129 to 80. Median budgets also shrank between 2010 and 2015 from $150,000 to $125,000.[7] That's enough to prompt budget committees to take aim at pastoral compensation. The result has been the surge in newly conceived part-time ministry staff positions that have become a hallmark of today's mainline Protestantism. This presents a thorny challenge for denominations and congregations that have long regarded full-time as the norm.

Continued decline, rather than new vitality, is unfortunately more the rule than the exception for churches that have made the switch to part-time. In the Maine Conference of the United Church of Christ, for instance, Associate Conference Minister Darren Morgan identifies about a dozen still-declining congregations that have gone part-time for every one that's experiencing new vitality after making the switch. In one synod of the Evangelical Lutheran Church in America, forty out of 180 congregations had part-time clergy in 2016, and the synod was expecting that number could jump to 140 within ten years. But not one of the forty was a vital congregation, according to a bishop staff member.

"Anytime one of our congregations moves from full-time to part-time pastor, we believe they're beginning the process of a slow death of the congregation," the staffer told me. The reason: a congregation needs a full-time pastor to be engaging the wider community on a regular basis. Otherwise it will not grow, serve neighbors, or display other marks of a healthy congregation. Even if this staffer is overlooking pockets of vitality hiding in the rough, the perceived dynamics need to be taken seriously because continued decline is a reality for many congregations that go part-time. This vantage from the field surely captures at least some of what's happening and why.

These observations resonate across mainline Protestantism as other leaders have seen it too. When they turn inward and focus on survival, congregations decline. Believing they're now too poor and weak to be generous to the wider community anymore, they close ranks. They direct resources, including the pastor's time, toward fulfilling what congregants want and need.

"For a part-time pastor, really about the only thing they can do is lead Sunday morning worship and visit the sick," the ELCA staffer said. "But in vital congregations that are having an impact on their communities and are growing and have increased access to resources, a pastor needs to be doing less visiting and more leading in engagement externally with their local community."

That death would happen for churches as they turn inward and collapse under the weight of their introspection makes sense. When their pastors curtail their roles as described, congregations no longer have a clergyperson present at neighborhood discussions, chamber of commerce meetings, block parties, or candlelight vigils. Congregants in these scenarios don't pick up the slack. If they attend the vigil or chamber meeting, it's not on behalf of the church. The faith community gets no mention or explicit representation. They abdicate ministries once led by the pastor. They no longer organize events that might draw newcomers, from welcome-to-the-neighborhood dinners to explorations of baptism. In these patterns of decline, the pastor does less and congregants don't step up to do more. Hence external witness to the good news of

Jesus Christ wanes. What's done instead is congregation-centered. The spiritual lifeblood of the church gradually dries up.

Plenty of part-time congregations, however, don't go down such paths of decline. They follow one of several alternative paths to thriving after full-time clergy, as we'll see in coming chapters. But before other churches can learn from their examples, we need to understand why so many opt instead to go down these paths that slowly lead to death—and why judicatory leaders often believe, wrongly, that decline is inevitable for congregations choosing to switch to part-time pastorates.

HOW THE FULL-TIME BIAS
LEADS TO FATAL DECISIONS

Mainline congregations begin with an increasingly untenable assumption that full-time ministry is always ideal. The belief contends that having a professional clergyperson handle a long list of duties on congregants' behalf is better than entrusting such ministry responsibilities to laypeople. In this lies a strong, one-size-fits-all bias toward full-time ministry as the model that's always superior, and any church that can afford it ought to have it. Congregations are so steeped in this bias that many believe full-time ministry is a necessary prerequisite for legitimacy.

"We were afraid we wouldn't be a real church" if the pastorate were to go part-time, said Ron Bookbinder, a ruling elder at Clarendon Presbyterian Church in Arlington, Virginia. He realizes in hindsight that this belief was unfounded; Clarendon made the switch and is thriving in multiple respects. But letting go of the bias and trusting in God to water and bless a thoughtfully structured, part-time arrangement took time.

Clinging to the full-time bias, rather than seeing it as one of several viable ways to structure a ministry, leads churches to make decisions that unwittingly stack the deck against a successful part-time pastorate. Judicatory staffers too often urge congregations to keep clergy full-time on the payroll for as long as possible because they regard part-time as the kiss of death. That's a mistake. In fact, the kiss of death involves waiting too long to go part-time and then poorly structuring the ministry to all but guarantee an inward-facing collapse.

Believing that part-time never leads to thriving, congregations in decline with full-time clergy tragically make choices that hasten their demise. If they're blessed to have endowments as my church was, they deplete those coffers by paying clergy salaries they can't afford. Monies that could have enabled future investments in ministry get used up, yet the congregation all too often has only pay stubs and no new flourishing to show for it. What's more, congregations have by then used up precious time. A membership that was at one time young and energetic enough to take on more ministry responsibilities in a part-time rubric is severely diminished in size and energy by the time the switch happens. At that point, fiscal margins are razor thin or the church is hemorrhaging cash. Laborers fit for the harvest alongside a part-time pastor are now few. On their knees and fearing closure, congregations in this all-too-common situation reluctantly go part-time at the last possible hour. But by then their continued decline is virtually a fait accompli due to poor planning, squandered resources, and flawed ministry design. When they fizzle out, they often hear: "I told you so.

Part-time is the kiss of death." That mistaken analysis misplaces blame and perpetuates the full-time bias in mainline church cultures. The cycle of death unfortunately and unnecessarily continues.

Along this path, congregations have opportunities to make better choices, but often let the full-time bias color their thinking in ways that don't help. That's where flawed design takes a toll. Congregations sometimes do as Holy Trinity Episcopal Church in Southbridge, Massachusetts, did the first time it tried to go part-time in the mid-2000s. The congregation didn't plan how laypeople would step up, and part-time candidates weren't promising to do all that congregants had long expected of clergy. After nine months of searching in vain, the church called a full-timer whose compensation package drew down the endowment to the tune of a $160,000 drop over eight years.

In other cases, congregations let the full-time bias inflate assumptions about how much in church life can only be done by clergy. Convinced that only clergy can effectively preach, administer sacraments, pray with the dying, visit the sick, and represent the church around town, congregations will shrug and concede: "Oh well. Too bad. Wish our church could do more for members, friends, and the wider community. But without full-time clergy, our hands are tied." That mentality distinguishes congregations that keep declining from those that take steps to empower laity in new ways and thrive as a result. Yet the mentality often proves tenacious because it's been baked into mainline cultures for decades. Learning that roles don't have to be so rigid, that laypeople have more authorization than they realize, that ministry in all its profundity and blessings is meant to be shared—all this requires a mental shift. Congregations that thrive after going part-time have made that shift. The

ones that keep declining after going part-time either haven't
made it or made it too late to be successful.

OVERCOMING STIGMA BEGINS WITH TRUTH

To overcome the full-time bias, part-time ministry will need
redeeming from the stigma that saddles it. That process will
need to include heightened appreciation for the important,
normative role that part-time ministry has played through
most of the church's history. And we'll need to dispel
baggage that unfairly saddles the contemporary notion of
"part-time"—not just in ministry, but in all segments of
American culture.

In many circles, "part-time" unfairly conjures nega-
tive connotations as though it were a synonym for half-
assed, half-hearted, or not really committed to the job. But
why? Dismissal of part-time as less-than-serious builds on
a flimsy foundation. Full-time refers to working forty of
the 168 hours in a week. That's less than 25 percent of the
week, yet it's valorized as if it were a complete commitment
in contrast to, say, a part-timer who gives 18 percent of
his/her entire week to a 30-hour job. In other words,
everyone gives only a fraction of their lives to work, even
those who are salaried and put in more than forty hours.
"Full-time" is a misnomer that seeks to carve out a separate,
elite class of worker. If our lexicon were more precise, we
would acknowledge that everyone works part-time. The
only distinctions are whether we work for one client (an
employer) or have multiple clients (as the self-employed
do); whether we do only one type of paid work or more
than one; and how many hours we work per week in each
part-time setting. Dedication is a qualitative measure of

commitment to work that gets done in an allotted time frame, no matter how large or small that window of time happens to be. It is not a quantitative measure based on the time frame's size alone. Hence those engaged in ministry on a part-time basis (under 35 hours) can be every bit as dedicated as their full-time colleagues. The part-timers are just working on the right scale for the faith communities they serve.

Reluctance among mainline cultures to view part-timers as every bit as dedicated as full-timers resembles America's cultural resistance to working mothers in the 1950s. The full-time bias echoes favoritism shown in the '50s toward stay-at-home motherhood. Though some mothers of that era worked, those that did were looked down upon, pitied, or both. Because they did not spend all their working hours solely on homemaking, they were scorned for being insufficiently dedicated to children and husbands who needed their full, selfless attention. This attitude was inherently classist, as only middle- and upper-class households could afford to live such a lifestyle, and glamorizing it only reinforced a premise equating wealth with moral wholesomeness. Mainline denominations, despite championing progressive public and ecclesiastical policies, have remained largely stuck in a 1950s' idea of a dedicated clergyperson. Expecting that the church must be a pastor's sole professional focus is as dated as insisting that every mother stay home and forego paid work in order to raise her kids. These days, some mothers still choose to stay home when doing so fits their families' needs and resources. Likewise, some clergy still work full-time when doing so meets their congregations' needs and resources. But just as millions of today's mothers need or want to work outside the home, countless numbers of today's clergy also need or want to work outside the church. This does not make them uncommitted pastors any more than working outside the home makes a woman an uncommitted mother. Just as America has embraced working mothers, mainline churches need to embrace part-time as a legitimate, holy, every-bit-as-dedicated calling and move forward.

Because ministry is not just any other type of work, redeeming part-time ministry needs to happen on a larger theological and historical canvas. The faithful need to know where and how it fits in Christian history. They need to recognize how their assumptions about full-time are mistaken when they believe full-time is how congregational leadership has always been structured or how it has to be set up if believers are going to do church correctly. Neither one is true, as a brief historical review will show.

THE PART-TIME IDEAL IN SCRIPTURE

Finding vitality in part-time ministry hasn't always struck church leaders as an oxymoron. In fact, Scripture sanctions it as an ideal ministry model.

The Apostle Paul was a tentmaker by trade (Acts 18:3). "I worked with my own hands to support myself and my companions," he tells the Ephesian elders. "In all this I have given you an example" (Acts 20:34–35a). He tells the church at Corinth that "those who proclaim the gospel should get their living by the gospel. But I have made no use of any of these rights. . . . What then is my reward? Just this: that in my proclamation I may make the gospel free of charge" (1 Cor. 9:14–15a, 18). Just as Paul identifies the unmarried life as the ideal to which some though not all are called, likewise part-time ministry alongside a secular job is identified here as the best way for those who can manage it.

Paul emphasizes the importance of being self-supporting when a congregation's resources are tight: "We worked day and night, so that we might not burden any of you," he writes to the church at Thessaloniki (1 Thess. 2:9). In true pastoral fashion, Paul adapts to each ministry context in order to exploit whatever structure is best to advance the gospel there. In more than one biblical setting, the best route for the local church is part-time ministry, as Paul does not insist on church compensation. He instead relies on his secular trade in order to foster congregational dynamics (diligence, gratitude, no resentment) that serve Christ's higher purposes. Paul recognizes that not every church can afford to support a pastor, not even temporarily. He suggests that financially challenged churches should not even try to do so. In Paul's letters, today's congregations find the biblical guidance and sanction they need for trading the full-time pastorate for one they can afford. Such a move can facilitate the emergence of virtues among the flock, just as in Paul's day. That's not a failing ministry. It's a church reaching a new level of spiritual maturity. Financial necessity just happens to be the catalyst.

The notion that a settled congregational leader should minister exclusively, with no other means of livelihood, doesn't gain traction as an ideal for centuries. Jesus himself plied a trade as a carpenter or builder, perhaps as a stone mason (Mark 6:3). Peter famously left his work as a fisherman to follow Jesus, but he returned to fishing at least sometimes after Jesus' death and resurrection (John 21). Those who followed a call to withdraw from worldly affairs and live as monks in the desert were spiritual heroes

to those who supported them, but not necessarily role
models for congregational leaders. Relying on support from
believers was certainly an accepted practice for all these
figures at times, but it would be a leap to assume that those
leading flocks were expected to do likewise or even strive for
that. Much like today, the gathered faithful couldn't afford
a designated leader who did nothing but tend to others'
spiritual needs. But that didn't stop them from worshiping,
evangelizing, and tending to material needs.

THE ENDURANCE OF PART-TIME
AS CHRISTIANITY'S NORM

The ministry ideal begins to fluctuate when affluence allows
one bishop to imagine a different possibility in the third
century. Cyprian, bishop of Carthage, oversaw several
dozen congregations in what was then the Roman Empire's
African center. With a history of nurturing commerce and
the arts, the city had bounced back from war and grown into
a renewed economic powerhouse. The prosperous context
gave rise to the fleeting ideal that wouldn't catch on broadly
among Christians for another 1,600 years: congregations
being staffed by full-time clergy.

Cyprian posited that clergy should be freed from
secular concerns, dedicate themselves to holy pursuits, and
rely entirely on their congregations for material support.[8]
Even in Carthage, the goal was too ambitious and expensive
for all to fulfill, but a new ideal was emerging, at least in
a region that could afford to dream. The wealthiest of the
wealthy would do things differently. They would free up a
clergyman to live an unimpeded, undistracted spiritual life
in service to his flock. Other Christians would hear about

what the richest of the rich were up to in Carthage. Some would aspire to follow suit, at least in their fantasies. The ideal rarely became anything more than a pipedream in the ancient world for the same reason that full-time ministry is getting rarer in our time: congregations simply could not afford it.

As centuries passed, ministry evolved such that congregational clergy were permitted, even expected, to earn a living outside the church. Throughout the Middle Ages, the priesthood was not a profession that could be used to earn a gainful living. It was a status, much like being a married person or a landowner. It came with prestige and power, but priests nevertheless performed their priestly functions in addition to their day-to-day work. They were frequently employed in fields that required some education, such as clerks, magistrates, and lawyers.[9] Even monks with clergy status held other jobs in their monasteries. Being able to consecrate elements didn't exempt monks from duties in the gardens or kitchen. The prospect that clergy would be trained in graduate schools, credentialed and employed as full-time professionals—on par with teachers, lawyers, and doctors—and then serve one to a congregation did not take off in the United States until the nineteenth century.[10] Until then, congregations in several denominations routinely shared clergy with other local churches, just as they increasingly do today.[11]

That's not to say denominations gave up entirely on the Cyprianic ideal of every congregation having its own full-time clergyperson. After the Protestant Reformation, certain churches felt a need for highly trained pastors immersed in the study of biblical Hebrew and Greek and in the local application of God's Word. In North America, Congregationalists and Presbyterians were the most determined to have pastors tethered to one congregation with no secular duties.[12]

But once again, economic realities got in the way. Only the well-off few could retain their own clergyperson.

A number of Presbyterian and Anglican congregations among others had to share their clergy with other local churches. The Methodist tradition of using circuit-riding preachers emerged in this context of clergy scarcity. Congregations would host clergy only about once a month, sometimes less often, as thinly stretched Methodist preachers spent the rest of their time going from one settlement to the next on horseback, bringing the Word to as many places as they could reach. Baptists solved the problem by setting aside gifted laypersons to be preachers at the same time as they attended to their farms. Lutherans often had to wait for mission preachers from Europe, who proved to be in short supply. German Reformed churches had to share their clergy with scores of other congregations of Calvinists from Germany.

In a society where clergy were routinely in short supply, laity often took responsibility for spiritual formation. Parents catechized their children. In Anglican and Lutheran churches, lay adults could baptize the dying in urgent situations when no clergy were around. Praying with the sick and dying sometimes fell to laypeople in isolated settlements, as did building up the souls of the indigent, the incarcerated, and the mentally ill. Rather than neglect such ministries because no clergy could be obtained, laypeople embraced them as their own temporary domains where virtues might take root and flourish. With some struggle and more than a little imperfection, they passed down a measure of know-how in the ministry arts to rising generations. The ideal of having clergy always at the ready was so impractical for some congregations that it remained a dream, not an expectation.

Reliance on full-time clergy became more commonplace in America when Gilded Age prosperity made it a consideration in the late nineteenth and early twentieth centuries. Preachers such as Henry Ward Beecher enjoyed international reputations for packing pews, even drawing tourists. They used a soaring oratory reminiscent of the traveling evangelist George Whitefield, but with an industrial-age relevance to urban social problems. Buoyed by charitable giving from prosperous parishioners, renowned preachers could afford to be dedicated professionals with exclusive focus on the affairs of one congregation. In these large metropolitan settings, they carved out the model of the preacher-executive whose main duties involved addressing the weekly assembly through preaching and serving as top administrators with programmatic oversight. Other responsibilities fell to staffers and volunteers. Well-heeled congregations such as Beecher's Plymouth Church helped popularize this remake of the pastoral role as a specialized full-time profession.

As this model and its impact spread to other cities and towns, congregations took keen interest in what their richer Christian brothers and sisters were doing.[13] Perhaps we too could go full-time, they hoped, and reap the benefits, including prestige and professional know-how, that were apt to come with it. By the mid-twentieth century, spreading prosperity allowed more congregations to hire full-time clergy. Indeed, from the Gilded Age through the postwar economic boom, full-time was increasingly becoming a norm that many mainline congregations could attain and others aspired to reach. Having a full-timer was evolving from a marker of exceptional wealth and congregational status to a basic standard that every respectable large mainline church "ought" to have. The sensibility that says any self-respecting congregation should have a full-time clergyperson all to itself was taking firmer root.

As the use of full-time clergy spread to a wider array of denominations, locations, and types of parishes, the model evolved beyond the preacher-executive to become a more generalist position. Those in sole pastor roles with no extensive staffs came to wear many hats as part of their jobs as the de facto, in-house expert on Christianity. Full-time pastors became go-to pros for handling duties that once belonged by default to laypeople, from catechizing children and shaping Sunday school programs to calling on the aged and saying grace before fellowship meals. In an affluent society increasingly accustomed to service conveniences, leaving the trench work of ministry to a religious professional made sense—at least in settings that could afford such a luxury. But this meant laypeople largely lost touch with the art of leading others in a way of discipleship. Biblical literacy in mainline congregations declined as laypeople felt they could leave biblical knowledge to the full-time professional, whose job it was to know such things and who would likely be the only one teaching and preaching on it anyway. Laypeople became less and less adept at the ministerial aspects of church life, much as they and their neighbors were no longer mending their own clothing or slaughtering their own chickens, which prior generations had done with skill and comfort. To be able to leave all such things to trained and experienced professionals seemed to be a mark of progress.

But coming to depend so substantially on full-time clergy has fueled the crisis that mainline congregations must now manage. As churches return to Christianity's long, affordable tradition of using part-time clergy, laypeople must reclaim a larger share of the pastoral ministry at a time when they don't know how and haven't been expected to learn. Furthermore, the world has changed. Few have ample time or excess resources to learn lost arts, even if doing so would build up God's kingdom. Congregations are used to relying on professionals to be at-the-ready providers of religious goods and services that they can no longer afford to commission on such a scale. Like consumers during a recession, they need to figure out how to do for themselves and for one another what's needed in a new time. Except now they won't be approaching religious life so much as consumers anymore. They will be ministers.

"It's putting into reality what has always been the theory," said Rolfe Lawson, an Episcopal priest in the diocese of Albany. He was the guest preacher at St. Luke's Church in Fair Haven, Vermont, on a July day when parishioners broke into small groups during worship to divvy up among themselves what had once been the duties of the settled priest. In that, he sees the future—and an ancient church ideal being fulfilled.

RECLAIMING PART-TIME FOR A NEW WORLD

As congregations reclaim part-time ministry and learn to thrive with it, they engage a task more complex than simply plugging in a new staffing configuration. And they do more than just decide to start living and ministering as the ancient church did. The world has changed, and a reclaiming of the part-time norm will need to fit into the world as we know it.

Laypeople begin from a different starting point than those of past generations. Though many today don't have much first-hand experience with robust lay ministry, they have behind them a tradition with recent as well as older strains to draw upon. They also have cutting-edge skills and timely experiences with great potential for transferability to a church context. And they have in both Scripture and tradition a sanction to go further than they've seen their peers go in donning the mantle of Christian ministry. It's not just for clergy anymore.

Part-time congregations stand on a firm foundation when they recall the scriptural basis for deconcentrating the pastorate and effectively distributing its power among the congregation. In 1 Corinthians 12, the apostle Paul tells the church at Corinth how the Holy Spirit empowers the people for ministry. The Spirit doesn't vest powers solely in one person at the helm. Instead:

> To each is given the manifestation of the Spirit for the common good. To one is given through the Spirit the utterance of wisdom, and to another the utterance of knowledge according to the same Spirit, to another faith by the same Spirit, to another gifts of healing by the one Spirit, to another the working of miracles, to another prophecy, to another the discernment of spirits, to another various kinds of tongues, to another the interpretation of tongues. All these are activated by one and the same Spirit, who allots to each one individually just as the Spirit chooses.
>
> 1 Cor. 12:7–11

Paul describes a community in which divine power is manifest in various forms among a variety of individuals. The faithful can't just sit back and trust in a religious professional whom they hope or expect to be blessed with a freakish array of gifts: public speaking, biblical scholarship, administration, conflict resolution, counseling, public relations, teaching, personnel management, and on and on. A way truer to the Scripture would cultivate divine gifts revealed among the many, which is what we see happening in thriving part-time congregations. To recall that "those members of the body that we think less honorable we clothe with greater honor" (1 Cor. 12:23a) is to hear a calling for those who had been passively on the sidelines to step in and own what the Spirit has given them for the good of the church and the world.

In this prelude to modern ministry, a blessed irony marks the journey of mainline congregations into part-time ministry. Many went reluctantly to part-time, wishing they could afford what other churches have and what they themselves used to have in terms of professional support. But from the pressure of financial constraints has come the recovery of an ancient, well-worn model of ministry that has proven adaptable and resilient across the globe through the ages. Today's downsized congregations are learning they can let go of a full-time standard that might turn out to have been a blip, an aberration in the long trajectory of Christian history. Their moves begin with recognizing the gifts God has showered not only on their pulpits but also in their pews. To see how they thrive in a new structure, we look first at the revival of lay ministries.

Chapter 2

SURE, I CAN GIVE A SERMON

*How Laypeople Step Up
and Share Leadership*

When Christ Episcopal Church in Bethel, Vermont, had a full-time priest in the 1990s, the congregation knew it faced some tough choices ahead. Worship attendance in this economically depressed area fluctuated with the seasons and wasn't large enough to support a full-time compensation package.[1] Christ Church faced financial challenges in trying to maintain two houses of worship that date to the nineteenth century. Parting with that historic legacy was more than the congregation could stomach. Turning to part-time ministry came with perils and warnings that attendance might decline further, but the people of Christ Church decided to take the risk.

Christ Church switched to part-time ministry and became a thriving congregation. Church finances went from unsustainable to stable once the priest's compensation was no longer a source of constant worry. Christ Church has no staff costs now because its priest is unpaid. She was a Christ Church parishioner with a full-time job as an insurance agent and got ordained so that her church could have a priest. Being able to shift funds to property upkeep has helped the church's historic buildings get the renovations they've needed. Average Sunday attendance has remained steady in the low twenties, with as many as fifty in the summer, and new members replacing those who pass on or relocate. The

church gives around $1,000 annually to feed the hungry via
Bethel Food Shelf, a donation that never would not have
been possible when the church had paid staff, according
to Senior Warden Nancy Wuttke. Congregants are more
engaged than ever before as everyone now has at least one
area of ministry responsibility.

"It's up to us to keep the church alive," says Katie
Runde, an artist and musician in her thirties who joined the
church a few years ago and is now in training to become
another unpaid priest at Christ Church. "In some ways, it's
more alive because every member is active."

Christ Church's success traces back to steps it took
to free up and empower laypeople for effective ministry
within the Episcopal tradition. From the laity's own ranks
emerged its first unpaid part-time priest, the Rev. Shellie
Richardson. She traveled a custom education path with
guidance from the Diocese of Vermont's Commission on
Ministry to become ordained and serve Christ Church. A
few years later, in 2017, the congregation raised up another
laywoman, Kathy Hartman, to serve as a second priest and
help carry the load. But even before Hartman joined the
clergy, the congregation was mobilized to share pastoral
duties and make sure no one got burned out.

Labor at Christ Church, whether ministerial or
administrative in nature, is distributed to the greatest
extent possible. Rather than require the Rev. Richardson to
prepare a weekly sermon, congregants became preachers.
Half the congregation comprises a de facto preaching
corps as members take turns giving the week's sermon.
Members with skills in the trades have put their talents to
work reconstructing stairs and doing other projects. Others
with a flair for decorating gave the parish hall a makeover
by adorning walls with spirited, uplifting art in formerly

sterile spaces that congregants didn't dare touch in the days of full-time priests at Christ Church. Now when a vestry (governing board) meeting happens after worship, the atmosphere is joyful with laughs mixed in with meaningful decisions and open discussion led by a positive, high-energy lay leader. Laypeople have taken a large measure of control and are not looking back.

"If we were given some big chunk of money now, we would do more repairs on old Christ Church," Wuttke says. "I don't think it would even occur to us to say: 'Oh, you know what, we could probably afford a priest now.' Having a paid priest would probably free us up to do other things, but I don't know that we want to be freed up. We kind of enjoy feeling like we're needed and supporting each other."

In Christ Church's experience lie clues into what enables congregations to find new vitality with part-time ministry. The key isn't to find a charismatic clergyperson who's independently wealthy and treats the ministry as a meaningful hobby. Nor is the ticket to find a pastor who is willing, perhaps due to weak boundary-setting skills or the inability to say "no" to congregants, to put in full-time hours for part-time pay. Such arrangements lead too frequently to burnout and resentment. Congregations that feel they must have full-time clergy need to say as much when seeking a pastor, even if the offered compensation is uncompetitively low. As soon as a congregation ignores limits on a part-time pastor's time or winks dismissively at the idea of ministry being part-time, it is disrespecting the pastor's capacity to earn outside income or pursue other priorities. That's a path to exploitation and should be avoided.

Instead, the door to vitality begins to open when laypeople say: "We can do this. We can rethink the pastorate and take on pivotal ministries that used to be our pastor's job." As congregants imagine that future and live into it, they channel grace and impact lives visibly, including their own. In every situation that cries out for a part-time ministry to begin, insights from other settings can help a church discern the right structure for its own flourishing. Congregations can develop and share playbooks for succeeding in part-time ministry, even if their judicatory staffers are skeptical as to whether it can be done.

BE A MAVERICK: PLAN AHEAD

Most transitions to part-time ministry are not well-planned in advance. Bishops, conference ministers and their counterparts have told me that most congregations just sort of fell into it. They pivoted, or panicked, when the money got so tight that a new model was urgently needed. That's not entirely their fault. As noted above, congregations get bombarded with warnings to keep their full-time pastorate at all costs for as long as possible. They pray God will provide somehow for that full-time position to continue. Believing that planning for part-time would essentially mean giving up on the church, they don't plan for it. They don't map out how the congregation's priorities will be sustained in a new organizational structure. They avoid hard decisions about what will be discontinued to make way for the new. The congregation instead scrambles to fill gaps as they become apparent, even if the process doesn't make much strategic sense.

Congregations that thrive in part-time ministry often dare to think differently. They start by believing, based on biblical revelation and empirical evidence, that part-time ministry doesn't have to be their downfall. It could usher in a new slate of opportunities for maturity and growth.

They envision going part-time before the pressure mounts. Some debate the part-time possibility two to three years in advance. Once they've decided to go part-time, they give themselves a good eighteen months to fine-tune game plans and lay groundwork. That provides time for congregational discussion on how best to use the pastor's time; how pastoral responsibilities will reduce or be reallocated; and how expectations—both in the parish and in the wider community—can be calibrated to support success.

Congregations have been learning to make a road map before embarking on a part-time arrangement. Holy Trinity Episcopal Church in Southbridge, Massachusetts, drew lessons after its failed attempt to go part-time in the mid-2000s. Having bled red ink under an unaffordable full-time pastorate for eight years, Holy Trinity drew up a plan that would explain for congregants—and for applicants to the part-time rector position—what the congregation was prepared to do to share the ministry load. This allowed the congregation to develop job descriptions for itself and for the incoming rector, which was something prior priests at Holy Trinity had not had. In their letter of agreement, laypeople pledged to handle duties that would have normally been covered by a full-time priest. For instance, lay leaders would assess needs for new programs and ministries; monitor pastoral needs in the congregation; provide pastoral visitation except in serious cases where a priest was needed; and assume administrative as well as programmatic duties in coordination with the rector.

This level of planning helped make Holy Trinity a poster child for a thriving part-time congregation in the

Episcopal Diocese of Western Massachusetts. Unlike nine years earlier when few qualified candidates expressed interest, this time the position was filled by the Rev. Richard Signore, an experienced priest who was officially retired but eager for a part-time opportunity. He told me he'd been impressed that Holy Trinity was organized with a clear, viable plan for sharing the ministry load and for honoring his part-time commitment. The plan also helped the church discern ministry priorities while reaching out to its transformed neighborhood, which has become largely Latino and faces challenges from poverty to crime and substance abuse. For example, helping neighbors learn about free public gardening opportunities in the city emerged as an important outreach of Holy Trinity. Teaming up with bilingual volunteers opened doors to new relationships. Weekday soup lunches were phased out as they didn't seem to meet a need. Now the church has regular outreach and stable finances. On the day I visited, more than 100 were in worship, including a few dozen Latino family members visiting for their youngsters' First Communion experiences.

Now part-time congregations that aspire to be vital are being coached to follow in the advance-planning ways of Christ Church and Holy Trinity. That's how congregants at St. Luke's Episcopal Church in Fair Haven, Vermont, found themselves in small groups during worship with Rev. Lawson on a summer day, exploring which priestly functions they still need—and which ones they could still muster from their own ranks of about twenty active people. Five months later, Melanie Combs was called to be priest, which would mean keeping her job in town government, working with a diocesan commission to get customized training and eventually presiding at Eucharist at St. Luke's.

Other individuals were tapped as well: one for pastoral care, another for healing, a third to coordinate preachers, and two more for hospitality. Like other congregations, St. Luke's is putting its personal stamp on what a distributed pastorate entails, that is, when pastoral duties are not concentrated in one but shared among many. In the process, St. Luke's is also helping refine a pathway for others to follow en route to thriving in a context with downsized staffing.

START EARLY

It's one thing for a church to think ahead about going part-time. It's something else entirely to take the plunge and do it while the church still has many signs of health. But transitioning to part-time early, before a full-blown financial crisis hits the church, can be a ticket to making sure the congregation continues to thrive with a pared-down pastorate.

A good example comes from Clarendon Presbyterian Church, a Presbyterian Church (U.S.A.) congregation in Arlington, Virginia. Money was not a problem at Clarendon when it began a transition to part-time nine years ago. The sale of a church-owned vacant lot had generated $750,000 in proceeds, and the congregation had sufficient income to cover the salary and benefits for Pastor David Ensign. But the church needed to act early in 2012 for a different reason: pastoral burnout.

"It was killing me," the Rev. Ensign told me. "Everything fell on the pastor's shoulders, from running copies of Sunday morning bulletins to changing burned-out lightbulbs."

Burdened by administrative chores on top of pastoral responsibilities, Ensign had no time for the creative pursuits in art, writing, and music that once put a spring in his vocational step. Because his wife also worked, he could absorb a pay cut if the church would be willing to trim his duties. He asked his session (local governing board) to make him part-time as a means of retention and as a blessing to his health and well-being. The congregation said yes in order to keep its valued pastor. The church cut his hours to 30 per week and found other ways to cover what had been his responsibilities (more on that in chapter 3).

What started as a staffing adjustment, however, opened floodgates to other forms of out-of-the-box thinking and creativity at Clarendon. Laypeople realized that if the pastorate could be rethought, then so could other parts their life together. They removed pews and replaced them with comfortable, portable seating that could be rearranged to create a sense of intimacy—and no longer feel like a small flock dwarfed by its fixed furniture. Space without pews also enabled Ensign to playfully experiment with dramatic configurations for worship. The chancel became a space for art installations that change each month. When I visited, the space held Ensign's newest creation: a wild arrangement of strings, poles, planters, and names on tags to send a message about inclusion, immigration, and God's love.

After worship, parishioners told me how they too felt liberated by the way that their pastor had modeled for them. They saw it as a way of rethinking what matters most and bravely going for it. Clarendon member Ron Bookbinder said the move to free up Ensign's time has inspired him to take risks, such as going on a construction mission trip to help West Virginians rebuild after a storm.

"I'm freed up because of the new structure," Bookbinder said. "You're doing what you want to do. You don't have to get burnt out. You don't have to do everything. It opens you up to consider doing something different."

What happened at Clarendon has been playful and joyful in part because it wasn't done under a growing cloud of financial anxiety. The congregation went part-time on its own terms. All could regard it as a blessing for Ensign and the church, rather than a hard pill to swallow under a cloud of financial necessity.

Congregations that have acted early to avert a financial storm brewing in the distance have found it pays to get out in front of the problem. In Gloucester, Massachusetts, St. John's Episcopal Church went from full-time to part-time after its last rector moved on. With a three-quarter-time pastorate, expenses would be more in line with revenue. But the relatively modest cutback wouldn't be so severe as to require much adjustment among the laity. Embracing new roles has meant, for instance, that laypeople rather than a priest now organize St. John's weekly adult forums, which entail Sunday morning presentations between worship services on a church-related topic and then facilitating open discussion. In fact, many of the rank-and-file barely noticed the shift to part-time because it was too minor to affect them, according to Rector Bret Hays, yet the move put the church on firmer financial footing.

Moving to part-time when the shift can deliver meaningful benefits and before it's a necessity gives a congregation a sense of control over its destiny. Anxiety is mitigated as the church realizes it has options and can take remedial steps. If fresh vitality leads to numeric growth and the congregation wants to scale up the pastorate, that option is always on the table as logistically feasible. Going part-time need not be a forever commitment, especially if a congregation acts sufficiently early.

For those that have already waited beyond an ideal transition point: fear not. Though starting early can be important and helpful, plenty of hope remains for the many congregations that aren't so organized or just fall into part-time for whatever reason. The genius of part-time lies partially in its flexibility, which can often be forgiving when it needs to be. Congregations that delay might need to pare the pastorate more substantially, mobilize laity more assertively, and/or reconstrue ministries more creatively as a consequence. But none of that is inherently fatal or necessarily precipitous of further decline. On the contrary, such essential shifts can provide the life-giving jolt that congregations in a rut need. They can still tap fresh lifeblood if they rise to the occasion by opening their minds to the new thing God is doing in their midst and hop on board.

DEMONSTRATE YOUR CAPACITY
FOR NEW IMPACT

Discovering new ministry opportunities can be a powerful antidote to the worry that some churchgoers bring to the transition to part-time clergy. They benefit from seeing early on how the part-time approach can facilitate new impact and how it doesn't need to be the step backward that naysayers have told them it will be. So here's a tip: make room for a new initiative that meets a real need in the community.

Adding an initiative can be as simple as repositioning a familiar ministry so that it has a heightened impact. This is possible for even the smallest, least-resourced of congregations. Consider the experience of New Sharon Congregational Church, a United Church of Christ congregation in tiny, rural New Sharon, Maine (population 1,400). With only about six congregants showing up for worship, the Maine Conference of the United Church of Christ informed parishioners that they couldn't afford even a part-time pastor and would need to look hard at the prospect of closure. But church members were defiant: no way would they close. They would lead worship themselves. Clergy would visit on occasion to provide pulpit supply, serve Communion, and offer consulting input on decisions facing the congregation. The path to thriving wasn't entirely clear, but they were resolute to try and trust God to provide direction.

Fresh energy came when the people of New Sharon did what their last settled pastor had explicitly prohibited: change the day for Sunday school. The church sadly had no children, and Sunday morning Bible education wasn't drawing them. The problem wasn't lack of interest. Area families were keen to raise their kids in the faith; many were homeschooling them for that reason. But for those not already attending church somewhere else, Sunday morning marked the only time when working parents could relax at home with their kids or take them on an outdoor adventure, such as kayaking, snowmobiling, or riding all-terrain vehicles. Such factors loom large in Maine, the second-least religious state in the country after Vermont. The former pastor had insisted that families make New Sharon Congregational Church their Sunday priority. Only when that pastor left, and the congregation became more lay-led, did congregants feel at liberty to move their lay-led Sunday school to Tuesdays after school. They felt they'd received a de facto license to experiment and were determined to use it.

The church school move to Tuesdays met a giant need in town for after-school programming. The church had no competition because no one else was offering any type of organized activities for kids. Homeschooling parents leapt at the opportunity to drop kids off for a couple hours of socializing with other kids from other families in a faith-based environment. Within a few weeks, five children were showing up regularly. Volunteer teachers were ecstatic. The young families' enthusiastic turnout felt like validation for their decision as a church to stay open and continue offering ministries in town. Laypeople swelled with gratitude that God had not given up on them. The Lord still had work for them to do, and perhaps do it more effectively in their case with less clergy control in the mix.

The advent of after-school programming in New Sharon has injected a measure of new vitality into a congregation that still faces an uncertain future. The core group of churchgoers has grown from six to twelve. That's hardly enough to proclaim revival. But with no staff to pay and other expenses minimized, the congregation has stabilized its finances at least for now, and attendance is going in a promising direction. In addition to growing Christian education for children, the congregation has maintained a monthly assistance ministry called "Pies Plus," which makes sure locals living in poverty receive a basket of practical provisions and a homemade pie to go with them. As the church discerns its way forward, it has learned the value of listening to neighbors' needs and experimenting to see what God has in store for a faithful remnant.

TAP THE PEOPLE'S TALENTS

When congregations transition to part-time ministry, their success depends largely on mobilizing laypeople to share the mantle of pastoral responsibilities. Those that thrive don't do so by convincing a dedicated cohort to add extra duties to personal plates that might already feel quite full. That can exacerbate burnout. Instead, they redirect the faithful to discover what's going to give them renewed joy in ministry as people whose gifts are truly needed and valued. That involves tapping latent gifts that laypeople haven't had a chance to use but will flourish more fully when they do.

Returning to Bethel, Vermont, can help us see how such dynamics enhanced thriving at Christ Church. Unwilling to saddle their volunteer priests with weekly preaching duties, Christ Church congregants looked to their left and right to find they had enough know-how and wits within their own ranks to fill the pulpit every week. Some of the preaching gifts were easy to spot. For example, the former dean of a West Coast cathedral spent his summers in Vermont and was glad to preach on occasion. The young artist with a master's degree in religious studies was also a likely candidate.

But less obvious prospects also proved capable of delivering inspired, biblically based messages. These included a social justice activist, who drew sermon illustrations one Sunday from his experience protesting a pipeline project among Native Americans in South Dakota.

A schoolteacher, who speaks confidently in front of a group every day, said from the start: "Sure, I can give a sermon." Soon the preaching calendar was filled without straining the budget. Now the only question was how to ensure quality when the pulpit is open to everyone.

Helping laypeople understand what's expected and how to improve is part of releasing spiritual gifts for the community's benefit. At Christ Church, everyone who preaches is expected to proclaim a message from that day's lectionary readings. A team that organizes worship makes sure preachers receive feedback if they stray too far or aren't effective for another reason. Those who do best in the pulpit are encouraged to keep signing up until the cadre of preachers is relatively fixed, but with room for some to preach more often than others. A liaison from the Episcopal Diocese of Vermont consults with them to ensure they're staying on track. Congregants embrace the challenge as a ministry and a spiritual discipline. As artist Katie Runde puts it, oversight from the diocese is "enough to keep us on the straight and narrow," and the flexibility in the schedule lets her sign up whenever she craves the challenge.

"If I'm in a rut, sometimes I'll sign up for preaching, and it always helps," says Runde. "You're keeping the congregation in mind while you're writing it. You have to reach out, not just turn inward."

Because it's not just one or two but ten who take turns in the pulpit, no one feels overburdened by having to preach too often. And congregants don't feel cheated by the fact that they lack a consistent preaching voice and don't always hear from a seminary-trained speaker. On the contrary, they feel a bit sorry for congregations that hear every week from the same preacher, who inevitably recycles favorite themes and runs the risk of becoming predictable, boring, or both.

"Where else can you go where you might have a different voice for nine weeks in a row from the pulpit?" asks Eric Richardson, a member of Christ Church and husband of the Rev. Richardson, who preaches only as often as she wants to through the year. "The variety is an attraction."

Not every church is blessed with as many capable preachers as Christ Church, but all have ministry gifts woven in the fabric of the laity. In case after case, congregations that find vitality in a part-time ministry context are cultivating environments where the laity's charism can shine. At Acton Congregational Church, a UCC congregation in Acton, Maine, the preaching is left primarily to Pastor AbbyLynn Haskell, who is either leading ocean retreats aboard a 42-foot sailboat or home raising children when she's not ministering part-time. But she gets plenty of help with other aspects of ministry, including from a congregant whose Stephen Ministry training equips her to provide Christian counsel to people going through difficult transitions such as grief or divorce.[2]

That parishioner hasn't always felt so empowered. She left another church because its full-time pastor insisted that counseling for those going through hard times was his job and his alone. He reportedly would not let her tell the congregation that she was available for listening and support. Feeling unable to use her gifts and training, she began searching for a new church where she could use her training and experience as a lay counselor. Now at Acton Congregational, she feels embraced as a valued member who can contribute precisely from the wellspring that she knows to be blessings, given for the good of others. With joy and purpose, she makes sure the people of Acton Congregational have a shoulder to cry on or a sounding board available when Pastor Haskell is not. Her outreach, along with other expansions of ministry in recent years at Acton Congregation, adds vitality to a church that has been seeing its membership increase with population growth in southwest Maine.

That's what laypeople do in vital congregations with part-time clergy: they move into roles they find meaningful, rewarding, and fun. They spread their wings in ministries long seen as off-limits to laypeople. In the process, pent-up passions get unleashed and channeled within a supportive structure that ensures accountability for the good of all involved. When this is happening, visitors to a congregation hear plenty of laughter. It comes from a place of confidence that it's OK to be themselves in this holy place. Tapping the talents of laypeople then becomes more than conscripting Christian soldiers to do whatever must be done in the absence of a full-time pastor. Of course, not everything is fun and less desirable tasks must be divvied up as well. But the emphasis is on enabling laypeople to delight more daringly in doing what they love in a ministry context. When they do, the positive vibe is contagious.

SEIZE MORE OF THE TRADITION

When channeling latent and unsung talents of laypeople, congregations need pathways where people and their abilities can be pointed. Then personal gifts can flourish within the framework of an inherited spiritual tradition and flower into blessings for the wider community. Those that thrive with part-time clergy do this in part by tapping more deeply into their denominational traditions. They encourage laypeople to do things their traditions authorize them to do, even though they've perhaps never seen laypeople doing them in that local church or in sister churches for that matter. What is customarily deferred to clergy in full-time settings can often be reclaimed by laypeople in part-time contexts—especially if laypeople learn what they're allowed to do and hop on it.

Reclaiming tradition can be energized by need rather than nostalgia. That's been the case in Henderson, Nevada, where neon casino lights dominate the landscape and nothing in the built environment is more than a few decades old. Here at St. Timothy's Episcopal Church, parishioner Muriel Dufendach undertakes a variety of ministries that, in full-time congregations, tend to be the customary province of clergy. She was instrumental in launching and overseeing Friends in the Desert, a six-days-a-week feeding ministry that operates out of St. Timothy's. Now when death comes for a homeless person, a veteran or anyone else who depends on Friends in the Desert, Dufendach officiates the memorial service at St. Timothy's. She also presides at two weekday Eucharistic services, where she feeds St. Timothy's congregants with sacramental bread and wine that had been consecrated on the prior Sunday by St. Timothy's part-time priest, the Rev. Carol Walton.

"Laypeople can do an awful lot of stuff in the church," Dufendach said.

The fact that full-time clergy routinely lead memorial services and weekday Eucharists in other congregations is of no concern to Walton or to worshipers at St. Timothy's. In fact, Walton knows her congregants are inspired by Dufendach's dedication, including times when the church was between priests and relied on Dufendach for these pastoral ministries. Together, priest and laity at St. Timothy's are utilizing lay ministry traditions that are relatively common in Nevada, where most Episcopal congregations have no full-time priest, but are seldom exercised in regions where full-time is the norm. Taking similar steps is possible in regions where part-time is increasingly common, but recovering such traditions can require a measure of out-of-the-box thinking.

"I'm not going to take over something that a layperson has been doing," Walton said, "because I think that's part of vitality: having ministry that people want to do."

In other denominations, reclaiming lapsed traditions sometimes means restoring more of the congregational witness in worship. In the Christian Church (Disciples of Christ), a history of frontier revivals suggests laypeople have an important role to play in shaping worship and testifying to God's powerful works among the faithful. But such dynamics aren't always intentionally sustained in local settings where full-time clergy regard the planning and leading of worship as their jobs to do—that is, as religious services that they are commissioned to provide. But those that turn to part-time clergy and thrive have found ways to rekindle latent strains of lay involvement that resonate in their respective traditions.

In Carlsbad, New Mexico, First Christian Church struggled at first after going part-time in the mid-2000s and then selling its building about a decade later. The property had become too large for the congregation's needs and too expensive to maintain. But selling it led some in the church to wonder about its future, especially after a merger with First Presbyterian fell through at the last minute, leaving First Christian to hold worship services temporarily at a funeral home. Discouraged parishioners kept their distance.

But average attendance increased and members got re-engaged as the congregation worked its way to a new home in a less well-off part of town where First Christian felt called to serve its new neighbors. Integral to stoking new vitality, including an increase in worship attendance, was how laypeople claimed a larger voice in worship and in guiding the church's direction. First Christian revived, for instance, a worship planning committee that had been inactive for years but was now drawing six or eight regulars to craft worship services. Sermons were no longer one-way monologues from part-time Pastor David Rogers. Guided by the committee, he redesigned his delivery to use an interactive format. Prompted by Rogers, congregants would voice their values during sermon time. They would share their Bible-based visions for what First Christian needs to be in and for Carlsbad. They celebrated their identity as a liberal oasis in a politically and theologically conservative community. They voiced during worship how much they love being a refuge for self-described misfits with tattoos and dyed hair, as well as for more traditional elders and anyone seeking creative ways to express the love of Jesus. Format adjustments enabled more voices to be heard while also giving Rogers some welcome assistance both in planning and leading worship. Letting go of clergy dependency and digging deeper into their Christian Church (Disciples of Christ) tradition made First Christian more vital than it had been when vestiges and trappings of full-time ministry still loomed large.

Sometimes the traditions a church taps when it goes part-time are more ecumenical in nature. Ecumenical partnerships forged among denominations might go underappreciated in full-time contexts but can have much to offer for part-time congregations. That's because

congregations with full-time clergy can often afford to go
it alone when funding and staffing their own ministries.
But those with part-time clergy are more apt to depend on
partners, and thriving can include partnering in ways that
build on ecumenical traditions.

Teaming up across denominational lines has
enabled vitality to blossom in the midst of an East Tacoma,
Washington, public housing project. Founded in 1985 to
bring a Lutheran presence to a perennially low-income part
of town, Salishan Eastside Lutheran Mission couldn't afford
to hire another full-timer after founding pastor, Ron Vignec,
died in 2013. The church called his son, Lauren Vignec, a
full-time financial advisor, to be its part-time pastor with a
mandate to do whatever he could to build up the church.
The new pastor made a radical suggestion: don't count
on him to lead worship all the time. Let him have time for
outreach, for building relationships and connecting with
people disaffiliated from organized religion. But how could
a group of fewer than twenty laypeople design and deliver
a weekly worship service? Their answer lay in teaming
up with their host congregation, which had long allowed
Salishan to worship in its building during off hours and had
always held its own services separately. Until now.

Combining for worship with Holy Jesus Cambodian
Episcopal Church meant capitalizing on an ecumenical
tradition that allows sharing of clergy between the
Episcopal Church and the Evangelical Lutheran Church
in America. It allows Salishan's Lutherans to have weekly
worship, share responsibilities with Episcopal laypeople,
and receive Communion from the Cambodians' part-
time priest. The arrangement has ushered in a pragmatic,
multicultural, Pentecost-style blessing to both communities
as they strategically leverage resources in a part-time

framework. Vignec still preaches once or twice a month, but not every week like he used to. That structure gives him time for outreach, which has enhanced vitality, as we'll see in the next chapter. After a period of growth, Salishan has now merged with Holy Jesus in all but name, according to Vignec. The newly merged congregation continues to grow its Sunday attendance as newcomers have joined and longtime Holy Jesus members now come to worship more frequently.

GET TRAINING

Sometimes laypeople have skills and backgrounds that bode well for taking on more of what was once the pastor's domain, but the transition needs support. A psychologist might have phenomenal listening skills and a nonjudgmental style, but she lacks the theological framework that sets pastoral care apart. Or a schoolteacher might have mastered pedagogy but isn't yet well-versed in Christian traditions of responsible biblical interpretation.

These types of situations cry out for training. It's only fair to make sure laity gain the competence and confidence they need in order to deliver high-quality ministry in areas that are no longer the pastor's responsibility. In many vital congregations with part-time clergy, laypeople seek out training commensurate with both their needs and their respective denomination's expectations.

Training has been a ticket to quality control at First United Methodist Church of Hudson, Massachusetts. Squeezed by financial pressures after a period of declining attendance, First UMC pared back its pastorate with no intention of reducing what it offers in terms of ministry.

To bolster its preaching support for times when Pastor Roseanne Roberts can't be in the pulpit, the congregation relies on two parishioners who've attained certifications for lay preaching in the UMC. Adult education programming is likewise not left to chance, even though Roberts isn't available to lead sessions. When the congregation decided after the Great Recession that a class on faith-based personal finance would meet a local need, it made sure the volunteers first went through a Dave Ramsey Financial Peace University training program before offering a personal finance ministry. Taking such steps gave clergy and laity peace of mind in knowing that a scaled-back pastorate didn't have to mean, and wouldn't mean, a decline in the quality of experiences that people receive at First UMC. The church saw a brighter future for itself and for Hudson if it could maintain high standards and systematize quality control while transitioning to part-time. Trained congregants felt good about doing their part to enhance the overall quality, rather than leave a vast range of responsibility on the shoulders of one full-time clergyperson, as they had done previously.

"In a church situation where you have a larger staff and multiple clergy, you don't feel that you're contributing as much," says a First UMC of Hudson parishioner who joined the church six years ago. "Here we feel that we're getting a lot accomplished for the pastor. The church is more than a place where I come on Sunday morning. I have responsibility that I like to have."

Even something as specialized as marital counseling belongs in the arena of trained volunteers at First UMC. Eight congregants have gone through Stephen Ministry training, and Roberts doesn't hesitate to call on them. In fact, she uses them strategically as go-to resources as she keeps her own workload manageable in a part-time scope. Example: when a local doctor whom Roberts knows referred a patient to her for counseling about marital problems, she determined in an initial conversation that the woman would need multiple sessions—more than Roberts herself could do. She knew a referral would be needed, and because her congregation had several trained Stephen Ministers in its ranks by that time, Roberts could take her time praying for several days about which one would be the best fit for this woman. When she made the referral, she did so with confidence that neither the married woman nor her referring physician would be disappointed. Roberts could meanwhile stay within her carefully defined roles: planning and leading worship; meeting with committees as a resource and guide; and representing the church as a presence in the community.

As we're seeing, congregations with part-time clergy provide something different for laity than the usual fare that marks so much of American Protestantism. In these churches, they are not the same types of consumers of religious goods and services that their counterparts are in nearby megachurches, for example. In the words of Vicar Alissabeth Newton, who serves as part-time priest at St. Columba's Episcopal Church in Kent, Washington: "We are a community of practitioners, not consumers." As laypeople learn to value and seize that all-important difference, congregations with part-time clergy will make the most of what they have to offer—and what they delight in giving. That orientation complements and feeds off that which part-time clergy do in owning what's distinct and life-giving about their types of pastorates. To that we turn in the next chapter.

Chapter 3

FROM LEAD ACTOR
TO BEST SUPPORTING CAST

How Clergy Thrive in New Roles

When a congregation shifts to part-time clergy, one question looms exceptionally large: what will be the pastor's role? For generations, congregants thought they knew the answer. The pastor would lead worship and preach weekly, provide pastoral care, direct meetings, spearhead missions, organize programs, and manage staff. Now all of those assumptions must be reconsidered because the pastor's time is substantially reduced. He would still be active in certain ministries, but which ones and to what degree would need to be hashed out uniquely in each local context. Once the pastor's role is defined, it might need regular review; what was needed last year or last quarter from the pastor might not be a priority anymore. And whatever gets negotiated must be communicated often to the congregation, lest unrealistic expectations undermine the pastor-parish relationship.

Framing the part-time pastorate is where congregations routinely go wrong and put themselves on track for further decline. Some fail to clarify the role. They forget that every church member brings expectations, forged over years in a full-time context, regarding what the pastor should do and be for the congregation. Congregations that keep declining have seldom done this necessary work of revamping expectations, and when parishioners get disappointed, they stop coming to church. Other congregations stumble into part-time without planning and consequently frame the pastorate too reactively and narrowly. Defaulting to a consumeristic mode as Americans are wont to do, congregants assess what they can afford and which religious goods and services they want their pastor to provide for them. The result is a shrunken pastorate that's tailored to their idiosyncratic tastes and designed to tune out what the wider community needs and wants. From such flawed designs flows predictable results: congregations that don't attract new participants and engage their members as religious consumers who are trying, not always successfully, to be happy with less. Decline continues as the lifeblood of vitality dries up.

Thriving congregations with part-time clergy design their pastorates intentionally to foster vitality. The models they use vary, but the concept applies across the board. They accept that the shift to part-time is not a mere tweak to staffing levels. Nor is it a change that the congregation might, with any luck, not notice if the clergyperson continues to don vestments and face the congregation each Sunday as ever before. It is a shift with profound implications for how the congregation organizes itself and works out its vocation. The clergy position is therefore restructured strategically to nurture and leverage spiritual gifts wherever they might crop up. Congregations deploy the part-time pastorate like an asset that's been recovered from a prior mission and can now be repurposed, like a room that once housed small children but now works perfectly as an empty nester's home office. Recognizing the pastorate as a malleable instrument in God's hands for today's mission is a distinguishing trait of part-time congregations that thrive.

To help these churches flourish, pastors need to find one or more ministry models that give them and their congregations a mental container for understanding what they're doing together. Such models help them stay grounded in the truth that part-time can deliver exactly what they need, including greater flexibility and democratized opportunity, in order to flourish as a mature faith community at a new stage of life. Getting to that place of owning the right mental models can be a process. Following steps that have worked for other churches might provide a useful guide.

KNOW WHAT THIS IS AND WANT IT

Even before looking at part-time ministry models, congregations need to lay a foundation for success that begins with knowing what to expect—and not expect. Seeking a part-time pastor should not be a hunt for a hero who will provide full-time ministry for part-time wages. A healthy, thriving congregation with part-time clergy accepts the pastor's limits and lives into its potential as laypeople discover they *don't need* a pastor hero. What they need instead is to become ministers. Part-time pastors help them get there by honoring their own limits and letting laity step up. Congregations should expect that God will send the right person who is attracted to this type of ministry. In other words, don't sugarcoat it. Don't try to draw candidates with hopes that this might become a full-time position. That angle will attract the wrong people who don't really want or feel called to this type of ministry. Expect that the right person will be revealed, perhaps by unexpected means—maybe even from within the congregation. If that person can't do everything the church is used to, that need not be a stop sign. It might signal that it's time for a pastor who will remove the training wheels and let parishioners ride.

Because a thriving part-time ministry needs a pastor with a heart for serving part-time, no pastor should be required to go part-time. A congregation exploring a move from full-time to part-time needs to listen carefully to the heart of its full-time pastor. Does she feel called to go part-time and have more time for other pursuits? Or might such a move cause financial hardship or excessive stress? If the pastor doesn't want to go part-time, the congregation should explore options. It might establish a yoked arrangement with another church and together cover the equivalent of full-time compensation. Or the church could help the pastor find another full-time position elsewhere and provide ample notice, such as eighteen or twenty-four months. If the pastor plans to retire or move on soon, that could be the time to go part-time. No matter how a congregation does it, the new pastor needs to be *voluntarily* part-time, not bitter or resentful over it, if thriving is to be in that church's future.

For the ministry to be truly voluntary, clergy need to know what type of ministry this is—and how it differs from full-time. A joyful part-time pastor delights in seeing congregants discover a love and gift for the ministry arts, including those long believed to be the province of clergy. Where a full-time pastor savors the experience of providing what only he can give—a finely crafted sermon series, a Lenten course on early Christian saints—the part-timer is more geared to finding where parishioners shine and putting their lamps on lampstands for the first time. If an Oscar were awarded for part-time ministry, the category would be best supporting cast. For pastors who believe in Martin Luther's notion of the "priesthood of all believers," part-time ministry can be the right venue to bring it to fruition.

Thriving congregations also need part-time clergy who aren't financially stressed to the point that they can't minister effectively. A caveat might be in order: Christianity has long esteemed those who take vows of poverty, and some who live frugally might be able to get by solely on part-time compensation, but that's neither a norm nor an ideal for today. Clergy who are thrilled to be in part-time ministry usually have other supports that make it possible. Financially enabling factors might include a pension from a prior career; a benefits package through a spouse's employment; a second job; an income-producing business; an investment portfolio and/or government benefits through Medicare. These pastors generally aren't counting on part-time ministry in a single congregation to deliver financial security for a young and growing family. They're clear-eyed about what it is: an opportunity to serve God's people in a special way while maintaining a rich life outside the church.

In healthy settings, part-time clergy have plenty of time for non-church pursuits. They express none of the guilt that often burdens full-time pastors when they take time for recreation or other time away. This suggests that part-time works best for those clergy with non-church passions that require substantial time to pursue. They indeed cherish that time and don't regret how limited their church hours are. I've seen inspiring examples. In Gloucester, Massachusetts, UCC Pastor Tom Bentley devotes much of his week to his other paid work directing a nonprofit program for the homeless. In Llano, Texas, the Rev. Dorothy Gremillion enjoys retirement but also values the extra income and spiritual discipline that she gains via part-time ministry at Grace Episcopal Church. In Arlington, Virginia, Pastor David Ensign delves for hours into songwriting, filmmaking, and other joys for his creative mind. In Tacoma, Washington, Lutheran Church of Christ the King Pastor Peter Mohr finds that being a bartender at a bowling alley gives him just the change of pace he needs from church life.

What a pastor relishes doing outside the church doesn't very much matter, as long as it's suitable for a man or woman of the cloth. Perhaps a prerequisite for serving a part-time congregation should be a strong awareness of how the position would let you, the clergyperson, flourish as a well-rounded human being who enjoys a robust, meaningful life outside of one congregation. Then, if it's your calling and you can make the numbers work, a congregation that's ready to thrive is apt to await you.

THINK IN TERMS OF MODELS

Part-time pastors can help themselves and their congregations by framing their work within one or more motifs. These mental models provide a bendable box in which to think about the pastor's role at a time in a congregation's life when conceptualization is crucial. In the absence of clear, agreed-upon motifs, congregants and pastors are disposed to flounder. They wonder: What are we doing? Isn't the pastor supposed to do X, Y, and Z like our pastors always used to do? What is it that we have now—half a pastor? What's half a pastor anyway? Does that mean everything gets done around here in a half-hearted way from now on?

Or does only half of everything get done because that's all we can afford nowadays? Without a box to give everyone a comforting reference point for how things work now, congregations run a risk of devolving into cesspools of anxiety and discontent. It's better to have a motif box, even if it's one that needs to be modified or replaced when it doesn't fit the situation anymore.

A model can provide a rubric for churchgoers to recognize and affirm what their pastor is doing, intentionally and strategically, with the precious hours that she has for part-time ministry. Many will be familiar with some version of the idea that a person has one overarching role in a system and might don other "hats," or sub-roles, as needed. For example, one person who serves as President of the United States might feel a duty to be America's spiritual and emotional leader in addition to overseeing the federal government's executive branch. Another U.S. president, however, might adopt a more technocratic motif, while a third might emphasize during wartime how a president must function first and foremost as commander-in-chief of the armed forces. In each case, the leader is giving the constituent a rubric for understanding how the role is being interpreted. It lets the constituent say: "There goes our president, being the spiritual/technocratic/military leader whom we've heard before. I have a category in my mind where I can file this. I understand what I'm seeing and why it looks this way."

In vital congregations with part-time clergy, three pastorate models have emerged: pastor as equipper, pastor as ambassador, and pastor as multi-staff team member. They're not mutually exclusive; more than one can be operational at once. But the rubrics help nonetheless to categorize how a pastor's time is used strategically to advance one or more elements that comprise vitality in a congregation.

Modeling keeps the faith community focused on transforming the pastorate into more than a dispenser of religious goods and services. The dispenser model hastens decline for at least two main reasons. First, it leaves the pastor no time for the outreach, community partnerships, and networking that boost vitality, as one ELCA associate previously observed. Second, it keeps laypeople so clergy-dependent and fed in consumeristic fashion that laypeople, too, neglect vitality-boosting activities such as spearheading mission or evangelism. With pastor and laity trapped in a bare-bones, provider-consumer complex, seeds of new vitality fail to germinate and sprout. Outreach, partnering, and networking seem unnecessary in the dispenser model. A better way is to reject the dispenser model and instead leverage the pastorate strategically to advance dynamics that lead to vitality. Buying into a model that's been helpful in other vital congregations with part-time clergy can be a valuable first step in that direction.

PASTOR AS EQUIPPER

The most basic alternative to the dispenser model renders the pastor as equipper instead. It resonates with the proverb: "If you give a man a fish, you feed him for a day. If you teach a man to fish, you feed him for a lifetime." The equipper builds up the laypeople's capacity for effective ministry. Rather than spend time reinforcing the notion that he is the only one able to do a host of tasks, the equipper endows laypeople to do more for themselves and the communities. The model can in some cases function strategically to keep a pastor moving her focus from one area of ministry to the next, each time enabling a group or individual to minister more competently and joyfully in a particular domain. By the end of each year, skill sets are distributed more widely across the congregation. Capacity is no longer vested principally in one ordained individual. Instead it matters less and less over time that the pastor is absent for meetings or programs that the prior pastor always led. In the equipper model, congregants leverage what they're continually being equipped to do. As they grow their impact in one area, the pastor can focus elsewhere. He in turn gains bandwidth to make different types of contributions from year to year.

Where the equipper focuses will depend on what the community needs. In Gloucester, Massachusetts, evangelism training for laity marked a logical place for the Rev. Bret Hays to focus some of his energies. He had accepted a call to serve three-quarter time as rector of St. John's Episcopal Church, one of three mainline congregations led by part-time clergy on the same down-town block. Being limited to about 30 hours meant he would need to work with the vestry to scale back and modify the job description from what it had been. Evangelism always used to be the rector's job. He would take time to be a presence around this commercial fishing town, which has no shortage of needs as residents contend with perennial challenges such as homelessness, substance abuse, and financial dry spells. Inviting neighbors to worship and follow Jesus came with the full-time rector's territory. But Hays pushed back on the assumption that it should be solely his job. He noted that Massachusetts continues to reel and resent organized religion in the wake of the clergy sexual abuse crisis that first came to light in the Roman Catholic Archdiocese of Boston. It's also the third least religious state in the U.S.[1] In this environment, Hays believes a come-to-church invitation from a layperson counts for more than one that comes from a church professional. What's more, he has much else to keep him occupied in a church that's still accustomed to a lot of clergy assistance and leadership. But the people didn't know how to do evangelism. They had never been trained, and it wasn't part of their culture. They wouldn't know where to begin, especially in a hardscrabble fishing town where people can be bluntly outspoken about their disdain for the church.

Hays's solution has been to strategically deploy a portion of his time equipping the laity for the work of evangelism. He uses Martha Grace Reese's *Unbinding the Gospel: Real Life Evangelism*[2] as a guide to help congregants learn the practice of sharing the good news in ways that hearers will appreciate and find helpful, not hurtful.

"It's not just a matter of equipping the laity," Hays says. "It's also a strategy to respond to the phenomenon that makes an invitation from a layperson count for much more than an invitation from the priest."

Because the equipping model is versatile, it can build up the laity for more than outreach. It can also be used to make them stronger in their ministries to one another, which is crucial when the pastor is no longer the go-to, always-on-call, in-house professional who does all the spiritual heavy lifting. This shift to part-time has been a boon for Lutheran Church of Christ the King, a Tacoma, Washington, congregation with 200 members and 100 worshiping on an average Sunday. Trimming the pastorate to three-quarter time accomplished more than just reducing expenses at a time when rental revenue was declining, and the church could no longer afford to pay Pastor Peter Mohr on par with ELCA guidelines for his years of experience.

It also gave him extra time to earn money and experience a larger slice of life outside the church. And it caused church members to become more actively engaged in ministry.

Parishioners at Christ the King experience the equipping model on an ongoing basis. When I visited in 2017, Bible study was no longer led by Mohr himself. Instead, he met with Bible study group leaders approximately once a month to go over the material, answer questions, and prepare them to fan out among the flock for small group ministry. That model evolved such that by 2019, Mohr was not meeting monthly with Bible study leaders but instead equipped them with questions to start group conversations. Congregants appreciate that their pastor is still guiding their leaders, even though monthly meetings proved too time-consuming for lay leaders. Their experience speaks to the dynamism and malleability of the equipping model as its forms aren't static even in one congregation.

Lay preaching follows a similar method at Christ the King. A small cohort with a keen interest in theological studies comprises a de facto preaching team whose members take turns in the pulpit one Sunday per month. That arrangement gives Mohr time off because he doesn't need to prepare a sermon, but he still consults with the preacher of the month. For laity, getting ready to preach always involves an invitation to bounce ideas around with Pastor Mohr. Lay preacher Jennie Wallace recalls him supplying her with commentaries on Scripture and scheduling time to discuss what she hears God calling her to say to the congregation. Preachers have freedom to develop their ideas, but if their sermon drafts wander too far afield or divorce a passage from its context, Mohr does some tactful redirecting before they do damage from the pulpit.

He teaches the church's lay preachers how to prepare a message by communicating in advance what they're apt to say and how they might deliver the message. All who step into the pulpit have received a primer on what it means to proclaim good news, and some get extra equipping when it's needed. Mohr once met a nervous lay preacher at a bar the night before his sermon and listened to him deliver it over a beer.

At the Communion table, the equipping model at Christ the King goes so far as to break ELCA rules. About twice a year, when Mohr is off, laypeople whom he's trained to preside will consecrate the elements of bread and wine and administer them as the Lord's Supper. Consecration is reserved for clergy in the ELCA and most other mainline denominations, but Mohr believes laypeople can do it with integrity in his community where an "open table" policy means anyone may receive the sacrament. Before presiding, celebrants study Martin Luther's Large Catechism and discuss with Mohr what Luther says about the meaning of Communion. As they get more comfortable in the practice, he finds they become more assertive and confident as leaders in the church. He believes the practice is consistent with his letter of call, which says he is to see that the sacraments are administered properly but doesn't say he must administer them himself.

"Circumstances force smaller congregations into breaking some of the ELCA's rules," Mohr said. "What does lay ministry look like in congregations that have been having Communion every Sunday and that's part of their character and their DNA? What does that mean? Our answer to the question is: we're not out to break the rules here or tweak anyone's nose. For us, this is just a necessity of ministry." The equipper model can prepare congregants for anything their pastor is prepared to teach them. Hays, for instance, coaches stewardship team leaders on how to facilitate structured conversations about stewardship over a meal. That approach ensures that the congregation doesn't have to wait on Hays or forego meaningful experiences just because he's unavailable to lead them. And just as teachers learn a subject more deeply than ever before when they're called upon to teach it, likewise congregants are going deeper in their faith because their congregation needs them active in lay ministry.

"I feel really sure that God wants me to be a part of that," Wallace said. "Thinking about twenty years ago, I'm more comfortable now to step out into a role that I might not have stepped into. And I'm not afraid to fail in that role either. That's huge. It's huge that this congregation as a whole allows me to try something and fail and still be like, 'That's OK. We'll try again.' That helps me in all aspects of my life."

PASTOR AS AMBASSADOR

Sometimes the newly part-time congregation doesn't need equipping as much as it needs something more adventurous. The laypeople might already be spiritually mature and also well-versed in areas of ministry from leading worship to teaching the Bible. Now they need someone who can represent their congregation in the wider community. They need an ambassador. Though anyone from the church could do it and some laypeople do it exceptionally well, the pastor brings a unique cache to the task because the general public already sees her in that role. The church is visibly represented as soon as the pastor arrives wearing a clergy shirt, and clergy who don't wear such uniforms just need to announce their titles. The part-time pastorate is plenty flexible to accommodate an ambassadorial model.

A good example comes from the aforementioned public housing ministry in East Tacoma, Washington: Salishan Eastside Lutheran Mission. As noted above, Salishan congregants freed up Pastor Lauren Vignec by setting up Sunday liturgies and frequently joining forces with their host church, Holy Jesus Cambodian Episcopal. Vignec attends worship as a coleader and sometimes preaches, but preparation time is minimized. His fifteen hours of church time each week, which would have otherwise been consumed by weekly worship planning and sermon writing, can instead be deployed strategically to fuel vitality in other ways. In consultation with lay leaders, he has carved out an ambassadorial pastorate that gets him out into the community, representing the church and delivering a gospel witness across East Tacoma.

By taking the ambassadorial approach, Salishan is purposefully defying the pathway that mainline Protestant congregations typically follow into a rabbit hole of further decline when they go part-time.

"They think of it like, 'We can have a fifteen-hour-a-week pastor, because it will take fifteen hours to do all the things we want the pastor to do.' No, no, no, no, no," Vignec said. "The *church* should do those things and let the pastor do something to bring in new people to the church, however that is going to work. And there are a ton of different ways to make it work."

Salishan makes it work by letting Vignec be himself and engage people by doing what he loves. He's a competitive street dancer in the Northwest's urban scene. As a six-foot-five-inch white man in that world, he gets noticed. And he uses that visibility to the advantage of Salishan's mission. He leads an outreach ministry to a demographic that's notoriously hard to reach for any church, especially for mainline Protestants: fifteen- to twenty-five-year-old men. The event, which happens about once a quarter at Holy Jesus Cambodian Episcopal, is a dance church called Fear No Evil. More than 100 young adults typically turn out. They're mostly African American, Asian American, and Native American men with a smattering of young women mixed in. Participants compete by showing off their dance moves for judges. They also hear Scripture read aloud. During dance breaks, they pray and listen to a message from Vignec. Each time, he applies biblical wisdom on one of two pragmatic topics: managing mental illness, including anxiety and depression, and resolving conflict. Participants are mostly unchurched; Fear No Evil provides their only regular exposure to church teachings or to Christian fellowship. It's also a fun, eagerly anticipated event that gets them into church and off the streets of the projects, where trouble is all too easy to find. This robustly missional dimension of congregational vitality at Salishan would not be possible without Salishan's thoughtfully designed, strategic pastorate.

In the three years since I visited Salishan in 2017, Fear No Evil has spun off to become its own church. Its events happen more often now, about every other month, and attendance continues to grow. Fear No Evil has started convening small groups weekly for prayer and honing of spiritual practices. Though this ministry isn't officially part of Salishan per se anymore, the church's entrepreneurial pastor is still leading it with his congregants' blessing—and with awareness that the Holy Spirit keeps bringing new fruit in settings where others had given up.

Salishan's ambassadorial approach reaches other people groups as well. Vignec travels in person to homes throughout the housing project, delivering food and basic supplies donated through World Vision, an evangelical Christian charity based in the Pacific Northwest. Signs of God's love are not abstract for people in need when the pastor unloads supplies from his own trunk, checks on the family, and shares a word of encouragement or prayer when appropriate. When Vignec is not serving as ambassador to nearby neighbors, he's often providing a presence in other parts of town where he believes Christian hope is needed. The Tacoma area is home to five casinos, for instance. Vignec doesn't gamble but enjoys the stimulation from all the lights and sounds. He starts conversations with gamblers resting between rounds on the slot machines or with employees on a cigarette break. Just revealing his vocation as a pastor can be enough to get people talking about their life circumstances, personal hurdles, and dreams. Contrasted with the wariness and hostility that clergy often encounter in eastern Massachusetts, the warm reception Vignec gets even in Tacoma gambling halls highlights how ministry models must be adapted to suit each setting. In this outreach, Salishan has a further missional impact on the lives of the city's most at-risk and transient populations. This too is a function of the pastorate's strategic design to manifest a certain type of vitality in concert with the congregation's sense of where God is calling the church to go—and where to send its pastor in the process.

The pastor-as-ambassador model works at Salishan largely because laypeople make it possible. They anchor basic ministries—setting up for worship, coordinating with the other congregation, making routine pastoral calls. Leaders make no apologies for Vignec's outreach; they support and defend it if congregants ever wonder why he's not calling on them personally and not preaching every Sunday. The congregation's role in outreach might be behind the scenes, but it is critical to the faith community's success.

To follow Salishan's example, a church needs to assess whether its laypeople are independent and outreach-minded enough to use the ambassadorial model in this way. If they aren't ready for it but aspire to be, they could use the equipping model to bolster lay capacities until they're ready to free their pastor up for more outreach. Or the church can try the ambassadorial outreach model on a trial basis. If the laity flounder, the church can call the pastor back to a more congregation-focused role. Either way, don't fret. If a church feels lost with its part-time ambassador pastor on the loose, the model can always be revamped or replaced with one that's a better fit.

Congregations can also use the ambassador model toward ends that are more congregation-oriented than Salishan's. They can proceed conservatively in the sense of keeping the pastor in the pulpit regularly but then leveraging his other hours to have an outward focus with a goal of growing the church. This approach depends on laity being able to handle pastoral care, administrative responsibilities, and Christian education. Pulling it off could be difficult in a needy congregation that wants to claim all of the pastor's ten, twenty, or thirty hours for congregation-focused ministries. Congregants in such settings might need to be reeducated on the role of the pastor, the importance of lay ministries, and the value of sending the pastor out to build new relationships.

The ambassador model can feel counterintuitive as a congregation goes part-time. That's because just as the pastorate is being scaled back, the pastor begins devoting a smaller percentage of her remaining time toward fulfilling congregants' needs. Yet that's exactly what enables vitality to emerge in many of the congregations that are thriving with part-time clergy. Laypeople still get their needs met, but the pastor is no longer the primary agent. Congregations thrive in many cases by embracing this mental model and living into it with a spirit of adventure and discovery, keen to see what God will do with laity and clergy in modified roles.

This angle on ambassadorship has fueled fresh flourishing at St. John's Lutheran Church in Lakewood, Washington. After going part-time in 2012, St. John's saw worship attendance double from twenty-five to fifty over five years. The congregation's giving to mission projects meanwhile climbed from zero to 7 percent of the annual budget. Pastor Joseph Smith's creatively conservative use of the ambassadorial model accounts for much of its success.

The Rev. Smith dons his ambassador cap many times a week, whether he's on duty for the church or not. Smith works as a substitute teacher in the local public schools, where he makes a point to wear a collared jersey with Pacific Lutheran University on the front. It's a conversation starter, especially among colleagues with Lutheran backgrounds. He's active in the community, embracing roles such as nonprofit board member and president of the parent teacher association at his daughter's middle school. When people he meets in these settings ask what he does for work, he tells them about his role at St. John's, which helps them feel a personal connection to the church. Those with piqued curiosity might show up at church a few days or weeks later. Being an ambassador on this level requires none of Smith's working hours on the church's dime. It simply involves being attuned to the power of religious symbolism and the fact that church growth builds on relationships, no matter where they might take root.

Smith is an ambassador at the church, too, when he's there a couple of days a week. Many nonchurch groups meet at the church, and he's dutiful about stopping by their meetings to build relationships and trust. For example, he stops by and visits with Scout troops that meet at the church. When he invites them to the annual Scouting Sunday worship service, they show up with parents, grandparents, aunts, uncles, and more. When the crowd swells on Scouting Sunday, first-time visitors feel more comfortable, he said.

Smith has also channeled ambassadorial zeal by simply standing on the sidewalk and waving at commuters on their way to work. Some look at him funny, but many wave back or smile. The simple gesture sends a message that the church is open and alive, interested in the community, and eager to brighten people's days with a blessing that comes without a catch. What comes of such outreach can be difficult to measure but not impossible. By waving, Smith gains insight about who his church's neighbors are. He's been struck by how many commuters who pass his church are dressed in military fatigues. That tells him they're working at Joint Base Lewis-McCord; they're apt to be in the city temporarily; they're not native to the region in most cases and could use a church community to help anchor their families socially and spiritually. Such insights have helped him position the church to be ready to invite military families and connect them with retired military parishioners who can relate to their joys and challenges.

"There was no playbook at all" for how to minister effectively as part-time clergy, Smith said in an interview before worship one day. "Without it being a circus or too much of a publicity stunt, you do whatever you can to have people in the church because the critical mass is important. If people come into what they feel like is an empty space, they won't come back."

Just about any church with part-time clergy can adopt the ambassador model, at least to a modest degree. That's because the part-timer always has an extensive non-church life and can "be the church" in settings where full-time pastors are seldom invited. In Cumberland, Maine, for instance, Tuttle Road United Methodist Church Pastor Linda Brewster works full-time as a nurse practitioner. In her health care context, she frequently meets people interested in health-related causes. Her response: an invitation to come along for Tuttle Road's medical mission trips to Guatemala. Some have jumped at the opportunity; their participation adds energy to the mission and delivers an immersive taste of what faith-based mission is about.

Brewster also takes an ambassadorial approach to invigorating faith practices. Her congregation frees up a portion of her time by taking on ministry responsibilities. A layperson preaches once a month, which means Brewster doesn't have to prepare for worship that week. She has also broken with the prior pastor's practice of attending all committee meetings. And the pastor's load was further reduced when Tuttle Road UMC ended a number of ministries that were vestiges of prior generations and perennially understaffed due to insufficient volunteers. These adjustments have freed up Brewster to do what she calls "constant experimenting" to find what allows faith to grow in today's world. Because local families tend to reserve Sunday mornings as family time, she spearheaded "Messy Grace," a casual style of church that gained traction first in the United Kingdom and has been growing in the

United States. Known internationally as Messy Church, the movement had by mid-2019 grown to 2,800 congregations in the United Kingdom and 142 in the U.S.[3] At Tuttle Road, Messy Grace involves bringing families with young kids together on a Saturday once a month for a hands-on environmental activity (e.g., composting demonstration), a ten-minute worship service, and an early supper. The result has in effect been a new church plant, complete with rituals and participants who insist: "Messy Grace is my church community."

"We had a wonderful baptism," Brewster recalled. "We had a pool of water with some white ducks in it. People sang 'Wade in the Water' and danced down the aisle. They wouldn't have done that during Sunday morning worship, but for some reason they would do it on Saturday afternoon."

PART-TIME PASTOR AS MULTI-STAFF TEAM MEMBER

The pathway to thriving with part-time clergy can involve some surprising twists as congregations discover just how malleable and strategic the pastorate can be. Nowhere is that truer than when a church establishes its lead pastor as a part-timer among other staffers. The structure shatters all conventional wisdom that says: if you can afford multiple staffers, then you should have a full-time clergyperson. My quest led surprisingly to several congregations where the lead pastor played a role that was strategically carved out to complement not only what laity now do in terms of ministry, but also what other staffers do.

The pastor-as-multi-staff-team-member turns out to be a model that's allowing churches to harness precisely what they need from paid ministry professionals while still honoring the constraints of a tight budget. It works especially well in settings where two factors are at play: (1) laypeople lack capacity to pick up extra ministries when the full-time pastorate is replaced by part-time, and (2) the region has professional talent available to be brought in on a part-time basis. Congregations in settings that meet both criteria are apt to find both the stability and flexibility they need by going with the multi-staff model.

Multi-staff models are proving effective in congregations that could afford a full-time pastor but choose for strategic reasons to be led by a part-timer instead. Consider Acton Congregational Church (UCC) in Acton, Maine. Because the congregation's building is in good shape and doesn't require much expenditure, an annual budget of $115,000 would be sufficient to support a full-timer in rural southwestern Maine. But the congregation opts instead to stick with a part-time, multi-staff model that has helped the church, over the course of five years, to grow its membership from 100 to 125 and boost average Sunday attendance from forty-five to fifty-five. The growth isn't staggering, but it's notable and encouraging, especially for a church that was open only two months a year from the 1940s until 1979. Now it's open year-round and continuing to grow as Acton becomes more of a vacation destination.[4]

Using the multi-staff model allows the congregation to access the specialized gifts of five staffers, starting with Pastor AbbyLynn Haskell. A gifted preacher who grew up in a clergy household, Haskell offers her skills on a part-time basis because between raising kids and running a sailing retreat ministry, she doesn't need or want a full-time position. She's also helped make sure all ministry bases are covered by relying largely on fellow part-timers.

When I visited the church in 2016, a compensated layperson handled pastoral care and Bible study; a military chaplain worked part-time with the congregation's youth; a fourth part-time staffer led music; and a fifth worked as an administrative assistant. Rather than lament that their jobs aren't full-time, staff members appreciate how their church income augments in some cases what they earn on other jobs. Parents appreciate how the youth ministry is supported by a trained professional because many are unchurched themselves and lack the requisite time and knowledge to lead in that area. The congregation thrives by taking advantage of what a strategically assembled team of professionals and trained volunteers can offer.

Acton's approach wouldn't work everywhere because it depends on a set of supports working together. One member of the team needs the skills to manage others. Funds need to be sufficient to cover multiple paychecks. Those with the right sets of skills need to feel called to ministry on a part-time basis. All the pieces need to come together, otherwise the multi-staff model breaks down. And because it involves multiple paid employees, it's not easy to pivot if it isn't working out. Not as easy, at least, as it would be with the equipper or ambassador model.

Other congregations have used the multi-staff model to advance a different set of goals. In Arlington, Virginia, where the switch to part-time has energized Clarendon Presbyterian Church Pastor David Ensign and his congregation, a multi-staff approach has played a pivotal role. A portion of what the congregation had been paying Ensign now goes to pay a part-time office administrator and a part-time mission director. An administrative assistant works at another church; she earns extra cash by stopping on her way home and knocking out whatever needs doing secretarially at Clarendon. The congregation's mission director works a second job as a social worker and is working toward ordination in the PCUSA. By moving from one full-time employee (Ensign) to three part-timers, Clarendon has distributed the ministry responsibilities that used to be concentrated solely and burdensomely on Ensign's shoulders. The congregation now benefits from the passions and special gifts of three specialists who run little risk of burnout.

Clarendon's laypeople are also at less risk of burnout now because they're no longer swamped by business tasks on behalf of the church. For example, managing the day-to-day affairs of tenants who rent space from the church falls tidily to the administrative assistant. That arrangement spells relief for parishioners who had dutifully addressed tenant needs but came to find the joys of church life tainted by the headaches of property management. These laypeople have returned to what puts a spring in their step, whether that's adorning worship spaces or writing cards to the sick and bereaved. The multi-staff model also makes sense here in the fast-paced Washington, D.C. area, where laypeople are used to relying on professionals in many aspects of their lives outside of church and have limited time for parish-based ministries. That the congregation has come to thrive more fully as a result of the shift to part-time is undisputed at Clarendon, where vitality is seen in stable finances, spirited worship, and more expansive engagement in ministry.

For thriving congregations with part-time clergy, progressing to a multi-staff model can sometimes be more strategic than returning to a full-time pastorate. Pastor Roseanne Roberts has been making that case at First UMC of Hudson, Massachusetts. She has an uphill challenge because the full-time bias runs so deep in American church culture. She hears congregants insist that the church should go back to full-time as soon as it has sufficient funds. But she reminds them: she's retired from another career, she's happy in a part-time capacity, and she receives health-care benefits through Medicare. If the church were to go full-time again, it would be obliged to supply her with health insurance under United Methodist Church protocol. At 2019 rates, health premiums for one employee would cost First UMC $18,996, and the pastor would need to pay a portion on top of that.[5] Rather than waste $18,996 on health insurance she doesn't need, Roberts has urged First UMC to be more strategic with those funds by instead hiring another part-time ministry staffer to work quarter-time with children and families. The congregation could find someone with a skill set that complements Roberts' strengths and fills a targeted niche. She makes a strong case for going multi-staff with part-timers and hopes the full-time bias will not overwhelm it.

As these examples show, faith communities are increasingly waking up to the prospect that they could experience more vitality, not less, by making responsible shifts to a new ministry model with part-time clergy in the pulpit. Greater lay engagement, more energy, and staff diversity mark a few of the benefits, but they don't end there. Moving to part-time systems that facilitate spiritual vitality can also bring enough savings that congregations can shield their endowments from the rapid depletion that's been ravaging resources in a fruitless exercise to prop up full-time pastorates. For congregations that don't have endowments, shifts to part-time can prevent diving headlong into debt and still enable keeping up with necessary building maintenance. These ministry models demonstrate a few of the promising possibilities at the disposal of congregations that need to make a consequential turn to part-time. To help pastors and laypeople succeed in these journeys, denominations now need to bring their own capacities to bear. How that's happening, and how it can happen more effectively in the future, will be the focus of the next chapter.

Chapter 4

IS THAT A REAL CHURCH?

*Learning to Value Congregations
without Full-Time Clergy*

Seeing a path to vitality for congregations with part-time clergy doesn't come easily in many corners of the Evangelical Lutheran Church in America. The belief that congregations can't be healthy without full-time clergy is widely held. It explains why one East Coast synod associate tells her congregations flatly that they are choosing to die if they go part-time. It might also explain why, when I reached out to ELCA synods that have seen double- and triple-digit percentage increases in the number of congregations with part-time clergy, I did not get my calls returned. Though I left messages saying I wanted to hear about *vital* part-time congregations, not dying ones, nobody was willing to discuss a phenomenon that's largely associated in ELCA circles with decline and failure. Where part-time is assumed to be a sign of sickness, new life in the trenches can be hard for some to see.

But at least one region is showing how a denomination can adopt a more supportive posture toward going part-time—and get better results than regions that don't. In Washington, one of the ten least religious states in the country,[1] ELCA congregations are going part-time with support from judicatory leaders who equip them with strategic options for embracing their situations and enhancing vitality. In the ELCA's Southwest Washington

Synod, Director for Evangelical Mission Melanie Wall-schlaeger was quick to list for me three part-time congregations with vitality on display. She explained how the synod was playing a role with mission support. At St. John's[2] in Lakewood, Washington, for instance, temporary synod grants were helping the church rebuild its generational mix, grow its pastoral capacity to more than half-time, and become self-supporting with a part-time clergy model. Rather than give up on churches that went part-time out of necessity, the Southwest Washington Synod sees them carving out vital niches for themselves as part of the diverse body of Christ in a region leery of organized religion.

In Seattle and points north, the ELCA's Northwest Washington Synod is going further in helping congregations see new routes to vitality. Initiatives smack of the entrepreneurial culture that gave rise to the region's economic powerhouses, from Boeing to Microsoft and Amazon, as well as a dynamic ecosystem of tech startups. In the ELCA, the entrepreneurial flavor is experimental. One project hosts open mic events; another serves beer and food as patrons sit on reclaimed church pews. And in the congregational sphere, part-timers are experimenting with so-called parallel restarts. In these settings, new ethnic congregations are cropping up alongside traditional ones in the same building—sometimes with the same pastor. In one instance, a bilingual pastor serves part-time in a flock with Scandinavian roots. She devotes the balance of her time to nurturing a new Spanish-speaking Lutheran church that worships in the afternoon. Vitality is still more of a vision than a reality in the Seattle area's part-time congregations, according to Northwest Washington Bishop Kirby Unti, but the denomination is investing in their promise.

These ELCA experiences highlight how a denomination can wield substantial influence on the prospects for congregations with part-time clergy. Judicatory officials can either stoke the embers to stir a flame or stand by waiting for the light to flicker and fade. National and regional bodies have the power to lift up vital part-time congregations as examples for others to follow. They can clear the way for recognition and a self-perception of legitimacy in the part-time trenches. They can create frameworks to facilitate networking and learning from others who've gone part-time and discovered what's possible. They can equip congregations with the guidance and coaching they need for navigating church life without a full-time pastor. If mainline denominations are to frame a congregation's identity and mission, then denominational structures need to feed their quests to become and remain vital after going part-time. Denominations need to update their cultures and systems to embrace part-time and help congregations thrive by doing it well.

All too often, however, denominations don't seek out what's working in part-time settings or help spread those insights. The ELCA is far from alone. Mainline denominations including the UMC, TEC, and the UCC don't keep yearly data on how many of their congregations have no full-time clergy. In other words, they're not tracking the universe of churches that has unplugged from their respective denominations' usual assumptions about how churches are and ought to be organized. Because you can't improve what you don't measure, denominations are living in a costly state of denial.

Mainline denominations need to confront the cultural roadblocks that stand in the way of recognizing, affirming, and building up their congregations with part-time clergy.

Removing those obstacles would represent a major breakthrough for the thousands that aren't getting what they need because denominational systems are designed to support a different type of church that is increasingly not the norm. Such a process starts with removing stigma surrounding part-time clergy, and the first step in that involves removing fear.

BELIEVE IT: PART-TIME CLERGY ARE NOT A THREAT TO FULL-TIME CLERGY

Part-time clergy are arguably well-respected in their congregations—often more so than their full-time peers. A 2017 United Methodist Church survey of active clergy found that part-time local pastors experience lower levels of stress and hostility in their ministry and occupational settings than do full-time clergy, who also struggle with more depression and less spiritual vitality than their part-time counterparts.[3] Parishioners in all denominations can feel entitled to be hard on full-time clergy, whom they sometimes view as their employees, in a way that part-time clergy don't have to tolerate. Part-timers also have built-in boundaries that allow them to say their time is up. They don't have to be responsive to parishioner complaints for a duration, perhaps a day or several days. Full-timers can't do that. Congregants are therefore much more apt to feel entitled to call clergy at night and lodge a searing complaint or drop by the office unannounced with an over-the-top demand if that clergyperson is full-time than if he is part-time. And clergy do get challenged: one 2016 study found that 15 percent of United Methodist clergy serving congregations in North Carolina said a parishioner had questioned their devotion to the ministry within the past six months.[4] But I heard opposite types of stories from part-timers. They find congregants appreciate that their ministry isn't a livelihood, yet they do the work anyway, presumably from a sense of higher calling. One told me that when a parishioner found out she was unpaid, he reached out to shake her hand, saying, "I had no idea! I have more respect for you now."

In denominational life, however, part-time pastors routinely experience second-class treatment. Regional clergy meetings are scheduled for times when only full-timers can attend, such as weekdays during business hours when part-timers are working other jobs. We part-timers encounter condescension from full-time peers who say such things as: "I guess it's hard to find a full-time position, huh? I don't know how you do it on a part-time income." They will bury barbs in jokes to say everyone knows all ministry is full-time; it's just that some only get paid a part-time wage.

Part-time congregations aren't well-respected within denominational cultures either. They struggle to relate to what's offered, from curricular materials to workshop content, because so much of it assumes the church has a full-time pastor who can lead or be involved with the execution. They get stymied by administrative procedures, such as reporting requirements that implicitly presume a full-time clergyperson and staff will be available to complete them.

All of this begs the question: why? If congregations with part-time clergy comprise close to one-half of all mainline congregations, then why are these pastors and their congregations so awkwardly left out of the dominant culture? Why aren't they supported to thrive?

Part of the answer lies in tradition. Today's denominational structures were built in a mid-twentieth-century environment in which many more of their congregations could afford full-time clergy. But denominations have adapted in other ways to a changed world, such as by ordaining women and embracing myriad new technologies. The resistance to acknowledging and supporting part-time ministries seems to stem from a deeper source of anxiety. The rise of part-time hits uncomfortably close to home for decision makers in denominational positions. Once that root cause of resistance is named and quelled, denominations can become the supportive influences that part-time congregations need them to be.

The systemic marginalization of part-time congregations and their clergy stems from fear. Too many full-time clergy, both in parishes and denominational offices, believe that their work will be devalued if part-time clergy and their congregations are seen as legitimate and worthy of affirmation. After all, the thinking goes, if congregations think they can do well with part-time clergy, then they won't hire full-timers anymore. They fear a looming end for a profession that has meant so much to them, to their families, and to their congregations. This is why, when I posted in a clergy-heavy Facebook group an article I'd written on part-time and unpaid clergy, 113 comments surfaced in a choral protest. Nearly all the commenters were clergy insisting that full-time, paid clergy are essential to the church's future—and alternatives to that model are dangerously inadequate because they lack accountability. Built into this backlash was more than a little professional anxiety. I heard echoes of outcry voiced by dentists against letting hygienists do more procedures. I had flashbacks in my mind to physicians insisting that only they, not nurses or physician assistants, be allowed to prescribe drugs or even refill prescriptions. In genteel church circles, such arguments tend to be less brazen and more subtle, but the undercurrent of concerns are similar. Part-time is marginalized, cordoned off from the denominational mainstream, because it's perceived at best as a devaluing force and at worst an existential threat to full-time ministry.

Full-time clergy need not fear that part-timers pose a threat to their livelihoods. Pastors with part-time calls have a different skill set than full-timers. They begin from a more collaborative starting point and delegate more oversight. They also teach to laypeople more of the ministry arts that full-timers are resolute to practice themselves in communities that still need or want professionals designated to deliver religious goods and services. Part-time is a different type of calling for a different type of person in a different type of church. It's also an economic necessity in about 43 percent of mainline congregations. Full-timers would do well to adapt to a world that includes part-time colleagues as evermore essential to the body of Christ and the ecosystem that is American Christianity. Denominations can help by applying their own rhetoric of embracing people on the margins to include congregations with part-time clergy. The sooner denominations drive out fear and make room for these types of differences, the more everyone can flourish in concert with what they have been given.

GET ORGANIZED: GIVING PART-TIME CONGREGATIONS A VOICE IN DENOMINATIONAL LIFE

Denominations don't help their thousands of part-time congregations when all their resourcing is geared toward those with full-time clergy. Consider an example from a national meeting of congregations from one denomination in February 2019. Attendees packed a workshop on improving church security in an age when mass shootings have become all too common. They came to learn how to take affordable steps to prevent tragedies and mitigate harm when violence breaks out. For more than an hour, they listened to advice from the chief operating officer of a 3,000-plus-member congregation, one of the denomination's largest and best-funded. Congregations with part-time clergy were among those trying to derive useful tips. But they found it hard to relate to a church that has $93,000 to spend on nothing but security in its annual budget. The church officer extolled the benefits of a security presence, namely six police officers in uniform, strategically positioned at entry points around the campus. He generously told how a collection of hidden cameras can monitor worshipers without their even noticing the devices, but that wasn't exactly resonating either. In the question and answer period, some of the heartiest affirmation from the crowd came when an attendee explained how her church got a free security analysis from the local police department. That response underscored the need: people in the room wanted to know what they could do to have a big impact at minimal cost, not how to build a small army of police officers on campus every Sunday morning. Yet in choosing an expert speaker, organizers showcased only what's possible when money is no object. They also illustrated how denominations can be tone-deaf when it comes to recognizing which types of sources have the most valuable and transferable insights to share. It usually isn't the church with the bells and whistles that no one else can afford.

Denominations can enrich the entire church by

enabling congregations with part-time clergy to have their distinct voices heard. In the past, when subgroups have recognized that they have a special characteristic to share with a denomination, they've organized into interest groups to raise awareness of needs and potential contributions. Think of United Methodist Rural Advocates, the National Black Presbyterian Caucus, and the United Church of Christ Open and Affirming Coalition. Such groups gather under their respective denominations' umbrellas—often with facilitating assistance from the denomination—to recognize common ground, share ideas, amplify voices, and advocate for denominational policies. They keep their Christian brothers and sisters aware that they exist and bring a distinct perspective to the table. Few would dispute that having interest groups organized for fellowship and focusing of mission strengthens the body of Christ.

The time has come for every mainline denomination to have an association of congregations with part-time clergy. These groups would share, among other things, how congregations manage in a world that doesn't fit what's prescribed in denominational handbooks. They might discuss, for instance, how peer congregations find part-time pastors when they don't have the wherewithal to jump through all the hoops required by the denominational search process. By networking in these groups, attendees would glean how other churches manage to secure health insurance for pastors and their families when their part-time status makes them ineligible for the denomination's program.

Also imagine how regional and national meetings would take on a different character if this sleeping giant of a cohort were to stand up and be counted. They would quickly make it known, whether meeting in person or online, that they represent a solid one-third to one-half of all churches in their denomination. Together they would call attention to urgent issues that impact people's lives. In the United Church of Christ, for example, clergy are ineligible for life and disability insurance benefits when they work fewer than 20 hours a week in a UCC ministry.[5] Part-time clergy take on secular work more often than full-timers do, and in the process they incur a disproportionate administrative burden in the Episcopal Church. Canons require Episcopal priests to petition for retention of standing and to report annually to their bishops in writing every time they have a gap in church-based employment.[6] Part-time Episcopal clergy also lack the defined benefit retirement plans enjoyed by their full-time colleagues. One member of the Committee on the State of the Church in 2017 noted that part-timers aren't well cared for in part because they are neither present nor heard at national meetings where relevant policies are crafted and voted on.[7] The problem raises social justice issues when one considers that part-timers are more likely, according to the committee, to be racial minorities and people who, in the absence of full-time positions with travel benefits, can't afford to travel on their own time and their own dime to national church meetings.

These are policy matters that affect hundreds if not thousands of church leaders and by extension their congregations too. Yet they get little if any attention because these constituencies have no organized group to lobby for remedies. Denominations should accommodate such groups by conferring status and visibility. They should also propose that such groups be formed regionally. Representatives from these groups should be speaking at conferences to make sure part-time perspectives, including distinct insights, are heard. Being organized could be the ticket to getting those insights into venues where others can be blessed by them.

Denominations could also help this cohort of congregations find a label that's both accurate and positive. "Bivocational" doesn't work because it's clunky and leaves out all the congregations whose pastors are serving multiple churches to cobble together a livelihood from ministry alone. The term also fails to do justice to those who are retired, caring for family members, and otherwise not working in a second professional field. "Congregations with part-time clergy" is an awkward mouthful. It has within it the "part-time" descriptor that, while accurate, unfairly implies a "not quite dedicated," "lackluster," or "half-assed" quality that thoroughly betrays what part-time ministry is about. The best we can say about "congregations with part-time clergy" is that it tells us these are a different breed from those with full-time clergy, which is true. A better name for the category would stay true to the type and also evoke why it's special. I don't have a silver bullet, but they might be called something like "flat congregations" in allusion to the business world, where "flat" refers to companies that lack traditional hierarchy and distribute authority horizontally. Or maybe they could be called "egalitarian" in reference to how pastors and laity in effect share the pastorate; or possibly "Spirit-centered" congregations could convey how they're organized to reflect what the Spirit does in Acts 1, Acts 2, and 1 Corinthians 12. In these churches, every member is precious, as Paul admonishes the Corinth church to recognize.

> The eye cannot say to the hand, "I have no need of you," nor again the head to the feet, "I have no need of you." On the contrary, the members of the body

that seem to be weaker are indispensable, and those members of the body that we think less honorable we clothe with greater honor, and our less respectable members are treated with greater respect."

1 Cor. 12:21–23

Congregations with part-time clergy also need hope, and denominations are in position to deliver it—if only they would let the power of story do its job. Local churches stand ready to soak up inspiring stories from congregations that switched to part-time clergy and experienced more vitality over ensuing years. When the BTS Center, a nonprofit carrying on the legacy of Bangor Theological Seminary (BTS), created such a showcase over a convocation weekend in Portland, Maine, in 2018, participants from more than fifty faith communities hooted and cheered as speakers from local churches took turns sharing what they've achieved by God's grace after cutting ties with full-time clergy. They'd been craving stories that would in effect affirm for them: "You are not alone. Others in your situations faced similar challenges and came away with new missions, building restorations, congregational growth and more. You can flourish by God's grace, too." They were starved for such stories and received them with rousing applause, encouraged to know that they were not alone and that they could thrive. Their judicatories and national offices have not been lifting up stories from the part-time trenches to show what's possible and to inspire them to be creative, joyful, and playful in their circumstances. This is a costly omission. Part-time congregations in every region have success stories to tell. Denominations ought to assign staffers to seek out stories of vitality with part-time clergy and make room on platforms for their telling. Doing so need not be expensive or time-consuming. It's more a matter of will. Denominations haven't wanted to showcase these success stories for reasons noted above. When that changes, congregations will begin to hear, share, and be motivated by what's already being done not so far away.

MAKE SYSTEMS FRIENDLY TOWARD
PART-TIME MINISTRY

Congregations with part-time clergy need denominations to understand their needs and limitations. Their encounters with institutional officers should leave them feeling understood, empowered, and energized. In regions and denominations where this happens, collaborative ministry is blossoming. But many structures, from employment policies to traditional ways of doing business, don't reflect a grasp of what these congregations need or are able to do. Just as telegraphs and eight-track tapes don't cut it technologically anymore, administrative systems that cater primarily to full-time clergy and their congregations need updating to get with the times. Denominations that take such steps will be stronger as more of their part-time congregations experience vitality.

Denominations can begin by studying how their systems conflict with the reality of part-time congregations and how to revamp them. By appointing a part-time ministry task force, a denomination can do a top-to-bottom review of systems and determine which ones need revamping to make them user-friendly. The Episcopal Church has done this to a degree, but its task force looks narrowly at training for clergy in small congregations, which we'll consider in the next chapter. As important as that is, a broader inventory is needed to see how part-time clergy are falling through cracks in systems designed for full-timers. In the UCC, for instance, full-time pastors preparing for retirement have an easier time buying into the annuity program than do their part-time counterparts. That's because part-timers can't use monies they've earned from nonchurch sources, which is often the bulk of their yearly income. If such problems lie with federal regulations of retirement programs, then denominations should be lobbying for exemptions and partnering in the meantime with other entities that can help their part-time clergy save for retirement. Instead, precious little is being done on these fronts and others because denominations are largely in denial about the part-time wave. Taking a head-in-the-sand approach comes at the expense of clergy and congregations who are at the forefront of where mainline Protestantism is heading.

Denominations can do more to understand the trends impacting part-time ministry and how to make it a viable vocation. Research shows, for instance, that even though married male clergy are largely still working in full-time local church positions, the same is not true for married women or for single people. For those two demographics, the ministry profession is increasingly experienced in part-time settings.[8] Implications of that discovery require nuanced parsing. A married person can in many cases receive health insurance through a spouse's employer-based policy. But America's population is increasingly single, topping 45 percent in 2017 and steadily climbing.[9] This suggests the pool of single mainline clergy is apt to keep growing, and single part-time clergy who can't get health insurance through a spouse's employer or through their denominations need to figure out an alternative. I purchase health insurance through a state exchange created under Obamacare, but not all clergy will find affordable options through such programs in their states. They often won't find them through their denominations, either. In the Massachusetts Conference of the UCC, the least expensive plan for a fifty-year-old man costs $685 per month, which is more than many part-timers could spare from their paychecks. Denominations need to be studying how to keep their growing corps of part-time clergy from falling through the cracks and having to leave the ministry.

Denominations need to be looking at options for this and other systemic challenges for their part-time clergy. They need to identify pathways to relative security for pastors so that the part-time vocation remains a realistic and compelling one. Something as simple as helping clergy understand what others in their situations have done can be valuable, and denominations can go further. They can ask whether their policies still make sense, including those that prohibit a wide swath of their clergy from accessing denomination-based insurance. These types of questions need to be asked as the congregational landscape becomes more and more part-time.

Among the most urgently needed policies are those that would support clergy with burdensome student loan debts from seminary and dwindling opportunities for working full-time in ministry. Pastors who train only for full-time ministry and have no other line of work are caught in a bind. They took out loans on the premise that full-time jobs in congregational ministry would await them after graduation. Now those jobs are getting harder to find, especially ones that pay enough to keep up with student loan debt. In 2018, the average master of divinity graduate finished with a cumulative $54,600 in debt, but the average starting pay for clergy is well below the $65,000 they would need to pay down that level of student debt.[10] Just the seminary portion of those debts skyrocketed from an average of $26,100 in 2008 to $36,800 in 2016. The situation weighs on congregations needing part-time clergy because this crop of disillusioned pastors could be in their pulpits—and not happy about it. The fact that women are increasingly likely to serve in part-time capacities raises the specter that many of them are not doing so by choice but are instead unable to find ministry positions that pay as much as those held by married men.[11] Denominations therefore need to grapple with a moral question: What do they owe these ministry professionals, who took on debt as part of an implied social contract and now find congregations can't fulfill the church's side of the bargain?

The answer is apt to vary from one denomination to the next. I'm not proposing that a whole generation of pastors needs to be floated or even subsidized by denomination headquarters. Many part-time pastors like myself have found a way to make it work by piecing together multiple income streams and finding an affordable way to get benefits. But those who haven't been able to make it work might deserve a chance to serve the denomination part-time, maybe on a project basis for a duration, in exchange for extra income. Or maybe a denomination would rather help clergy learn a trade that they can ply alongside their part-time work in congregations. Even though denominations face tough economic choices of their own these days, they owe something to clergy who sacrificed for the church and saw their investment unrequited.

Some of the updating can happen simply by making day-to-day denominational business friendlier for part-timers. In the Massachusetts Conference of the United Church of Christ, for instance, an annual Day of Covenant brings clergy from around a region together for fellowship, updates, and reaffirming vows. These are always scheduled for weekday mornings when virtually all part-timers are tied up with nonchurch commitments. Because none of us can ever attend, the conference never sees or hears from us at the very moment when clergy are gathered and talking about what it means to be UCC clergy in Massachusetts today. We aren't validated, and the wider church learns nothing from our experiences at these events. For years, I've reminded conference organizers that dozens of us can't make it. I have gone instead to a weeknight event for those serving in specialized ministries, as opposed to parish ministry positions like mine. Most who show up at these gatherings are chaplains, which makes me feel marginalized because I'm not a chaplain. Most part-timers just skip it altogether. The problem could be fixed by simply making it an Evening of Covenant and serving dinner instead of lunch. I suggest this every year, and no one even acknowledges my request. The lack of response likely speaks to how denominations have trouble recognizing the distinct needs of part-time congregations or even believing that they have a voice worth hearing. This example points to a wider need for judicatory staff to ask, whenever events are planned, or input is sought: Who is not at the table? A trained eye will notice that part-timers are often absent but could be included with minor logistical tweaking.

HELP CONGREGATIONS DISCERN
AND LIVE OUT THEIR QUIRKY CALLINGS

For part-time congregations to thrive, they need room to be themselves—and space to discover what that is. Denominations have important roles to play by enabling and guiding such processes to play out. They can countenance experimentation and departures from the status quo, while also keeping them accountable to the Way of Jesus. Insisting that they tether to full-time norms can be stifling and demoralizing, but that's not what happens where part-timers are learning to flourish.

In New England, United Methodist congregations—by necessity—get to experiment a lot more than their counterparts in Texas do. And they need judicatory officers to bless their efforts. That's what the Rev. LyAnna Johnson found out when she finished seminary and proposed to start a dinner church in Texas, where she's from. Dinner churches bring together people who generally don't go on Sunday (at least not anymore) and convene for worship with the Lord's Supper incorporated over a weekday meal. They've grown in popularity in recent years, but Johnson got no support in Texas, where many large UMC congregations are doing fine and her bishop saw no need to depart from the traditional church model. Undiscouraged, she took off for the rocky soil of New England, home to six of America's ten least-religious states.[12] A warm reception from her denomination awaited in this land where only 30 percent of United Methodist congregations had their own full-time clergyperson in 2016, down from 45 percent five years earlier. She did an apprenticeship at Simple Church in North Grafton, where the traditional UMC church had closed when it had only five members left, and from its dry bones came new life in a vital dinner church. Now she leads her own Simple Church in downtown Worcester. Johnson is technically full-time because the New England Annual Conference supplies a start-up grant temporarily, but the model closely resembles part-time. It involves working several days a week outside the church; she designs websites to support her ministry.[13] All of it is possible because the denomination has created room for experimentation and revitalization of the remnant left from North Grafton UMC.

Being kept on a denominational "long leash" has also been a lifeline for congregations that just needed a vitality infusion. At one United Methodist Church I visited, preaching wasn't done exactly by the book when laypeople got in the pulpit. Unlike at First UMC of Hudson, where lay preachers had trained and gotten certified, this suburban church had not gone to that length. To give its pastor one Sunday off per month for outreach efforts, this church asked laypeople to sign up for preaching and just give it their best, prayerful shot. That approach lacks First UMC's quality control, but it works in a setting where congregants can't afford time for extra training and the pastor's outreach is boosting church attendance and spreading faith. By similar token, in Carlsbad, New Mexico, First Christian Church received blessings and a wide berth from the Christian Church (Disciples of Christ) to make unconventional moves on its path to new vitality. The congregation went part-time, sold its building, and pursued an ill-fated merger with another church of a different denomination. The group worshiped for a while in a funeral home. It traded the usual sermon for a dialogue-style homily with parishioners taking questions and offering reflections. Much of this happened over less than a year en route to growing attendance, expanding mission, and increasing member engagement in ministry. If these and other congregations had to stick religiously to a denominational handbook designed with full-time congregations in mind, they would not have taken the routes that turned out to fuel new vitality in their midst. Sometimes a long leash with a supportive presence at the other end is what a congregation needs to prosper.

SET AFFORDABLE EXPECTATIONS
FOR ORDAINED AND LAY LEADERS

As denominations take stock of what they can do to help downsized congregations flourish anew, they could help legitimize the overdue practice of paying laypeople who cultivate proficiency or expertise in ministry. For too long, congregations have paid only clergy and musicians who leverage a specialized education for the building up of the faithful. Laypeople have theoretically had advanced theological education available to them if they want to sign up for online courses in evangelism, stewardship, or Bible study. But if they're volunteers, they'd be uncommonly fortunate just to get their expenses covered. To think they'd emerge on the other side with a modest credential that lets them earn a small stipend consistently from the church is virtually unheard of. Pay is reserved primarily for those who approach one ministry area or another as a profession, whether that role is for a cleric or a musician. But a growing reality says congregations need laypeople to dedicate time to developing new competencies and practicing them reliably in a local church setting. To provide a stipend could help them justify the time required, away from family and other priorities, in order to minister up to a standard that a congregation believes it needs. If a denomination acknowledges this type of compensatory practice, it can incentivize more congregations to use it—or at least recognize it as a legitimate option.

Some are apt to bristle at the idea of paying laypeople to raise funds for the church or to evangelize. Shouldn't they do such things just because they're lovers of God and followers of Jesus Christ? Yes, and some surely will continue to volunteer in these areas and others for those very reasons. But other realities also press on modern lives such that people need compensation even for things they love to do simply because they can't afford to donate all the time that's required. This is especially true for people who live in high-cost regions where housing costs alone routinely consume 40 percent or more from family budgets. If a person of faith knows he can get trained and then earn a monthly stipend from the church, then he might make the commitment that boosts the caliber of ministry in a local church while still reducing costs formerly associated with full-time clergy pay. The message isn't one of reducing lay ministries to a mere "job" instead of a calling that one does for the love of God and God's people. Rather, it's recognizing that lay responsibilities increase with the shift to part-time clergy. These new responsibilities benefit in some cases from additional training, commitments of time to the church, or both. People can make commitments with less stress if they are supported in doing so. And churches have more resources for such support when clergy aren't paid as much as they used to be.

Like many aspects of transitioning to part-time, pay for lay ministries won't be appropriate or needed everywhere, and paid ministries won't look the same in every location. But it's worth considering that if pastoral duties are to be distributed more equitably, then compensation perhaps ought no longer be reserved only for the ordained. That idea invites examination of how congregations, including clergy, need to be theologically trained for the future church. We turn to that topic in chapter 5.

Chapter 5

LEARNING FOR THE MANY

*Theological Education
for a Part-Time Future*

Transitioning to a time when pulpits are largely staffed by part-time clergy means mainline Protestantism must now adapt to prepare leaders for their new roles. Laypeople need education in how to leverage their gifts and add new personal capacities to advance God's kingdom. With these lay callings to lead in specific ministry areas comes a hundred summons to stock up on theological context, technical insight, ethical responsibilities, and heightened self-awareness. Clergy meanwhile need preparation for tasks of equipping, evangelizing, and guiding to a degree and in a style that aren't required of full-timers. In short, all who comprise the local church have a lot of new learning to do as we recover proven pathways and blaze a few new ones in a still-untamed wilderness.

But institutions of higher education that have long served as training grounds for mainline churches were not designed to fill the needs that lie ahead. The distributed pastorate, whereby clergy and laypeople divide up pastoral responsibilities according to the gifts of the Holy Spirit, remains a foreign concept in much of theological higher education. Seminaries and divinity schools have instead concentrated resources on training one professional person to arrive in a local church with a dizzying array of skills. This person is supposed to be an inspiring speaker, thoughtful counselor, organized administrator, conflict resolver, manager, salesperson, youth mentor, and so on. The preferred vehicle for loading up this future clerical leader has been the master of divinity degree, which requires three years to complete as areas from Bible to systematic theology, ethics, and history are covered. It ostensibly turns the clergyperson into the de facto in-house expert on all things church because she comes to know a least a little bit more than everyone else on just about every churchy topic. The laity meanwhile get no theological training before becoming treasurers, moderators, senior wardens, deacons, and elders. This lopsided education model doesn't fit a world in which laypeople need a larger slice of the available theological training and clergy need a different type of training that both costs less and includes skills that part-timers especially need. Theological education needs to start training the whole church for the shared pastorate of the future.

Economic forces are driving theological educators to examine the sustainability of their education models. Since 2010, twenty-seven schools in the Association of Theological Schools (ATS) have merged, embedded, or otherwise affiliated with other schools.[1] Freestanding, tuition-driven schools such as Andover Newton Theological School, Episcopal Divinity School, and Lutheran seminaries at Gettysburg and Philadelphia are taking such steps to hold down costs in a time when master of divinity enrollment, and therefore revenue from those degree programs, is down by 15 percent since 2008.[2] As former ATS Executive Director Daniel Aleshire told me, prospective MDiv students increasingly can't justify borrowing tens of thousands of dollars when the jobs they'd be training for are part-time. Because the entire system is predicated on demand from students who foresee full-time careers as clergy, the theological education industry is undergoing massive disruption.

"The Industrial Revolution really produced the professional guild that we call clergy, and that's actually the thing that's breaking apart," says Cameron Trimble, chief executive officer of the Center for Progressive Renewal, an Atlanta-based nonprofit that does consulting for mainline churches. "The industry of paid clergy, and all the institutions that produce these paid clergy, are collapsing under their own weight because the financial model is so broadly broken."

Yet much as formerly full-time congregations are reinventing themselves in a part-time mode, institutions of higher education are challenged to discern what they will become. In many cases, they appear intent on achieving economies of scale in order to continue educating future full-time professional clergy. More than a few, however, are responding to where the growth is. They are learning to cater both to a different breed of future clergy and to laity who need something more immediate and practical than a survey of patristic controversies or the English Reformation. They are experimenting with how to do it cost-effectively and with targeted impact. Like the congregations they serve, they are figuring it out—and those that hit a resonant chord have something valuable to teach the rest.

Congregations with part-time clergy will thrive with far greater frequency than they do now if theological education evolves quickly to meet their needs. That begins with taking seriously the need to turn laypeople into reliable congregational leaders with particular pastoral skills, even if they're not going to become clergy. Finding new ways to educate clergy, with or without the costs associated with expensive buildings and salaries, needs to be part of the picture. The well-prepared will have learned to think in terms of vitality-enhancing models. They'll know how to discern spiritual gifts in others and teach ministry arts among their flocks. They might even be offered, via partnerships with their theological schools, avenues to learn a trade and earn a complementary living alongside their ministries. Then our denominations' rich training resources will be deployed to support not only the clergy profession but also the wider, expanding vocation of ministry.

DEMOCRATIZE IT: TRAIN LAYPEOPLE FOR EFFECTIVE MINISTRY

The dearth of theological training for laypeople needs to be confronted. Though courses have long been accessible to laypersons seeking to audit or pay out-of-pocket for credits, they've had little incentive to invest time or money for the sake of their congregation-based ministries. Laypeople pursuing graduate-level education at ATS schools tend to be in master of arts degree programs. These saw an enrollment increase of 18 percent from 2012 to 2017[3], but these are stepping stones for professional careers in such areas as academe and social work. What remains largely foreign in traditional theological schools is the phenomenon we need to see much more frequently: laypeople seeking proficiency in areas of ministry, not new careers. When considering the requisite time and money, they've been hard-pressed to justify taking courses for church roles that come with low expectations for laity. And that's if they're even aware that lay theological education exists. In congregations where I've served, the view is that theological education is something pastors get, and it prepares them for the diverse responsibilities that fall on their shoulders alone. This vestige of the full-time bias colors laypeople's low expectations for themselves as ministers. It helps explain why those with abundant gifts too often believe that mundane tasks are all they're able to do in the church. It also illuminates why laypeople often think that if they're going to make a higher-level contribution, then it must involve analyzing the church's problems as if it were a troubled for-profit business in need of a turnaround solution akin to what they've witnessed in their own respective industries. They don't always appreciate how the church is unique among institutions and in need of distinct solutions because they haven't been taught to think theologically. They're doing the best they can, but they're like house painters without ladders: their lack of appropriate equipment is severely limiting.

The landscape is fortunately beginning to shift and make room for the lay education that's needed for the future. Schools of ministry are cropping up and growing largely for the purpose of strengthening lay roles in congregations. In Maine, for instance, a void emerged in 2014 when Bangor Theological Seminary (BTS) closed due to the same declining enrollment dynamics that are challenging so many other freestanding institutions. With the BTS closure, northern New England was left with no mainline training ground for church leaders, but the void gave rise to something new. The Maine School of Ministry was founded by the Maine Conference of the UCC to provide low-cost training in specific areas for laypeople and future clergy. The Christian Studies and Leadership Certificate Program provides tracks for licensed, commissioned, and ordained ministries.[4] Similar institutions have been gaining traction in other denominations, such as the Stevenson School of Ministry, serving the Episcopal Diocese of Central Pennsylvania. By utilizing an existing, no-frills space that churches already have and faculty who aren't depending on the work to afford them a full-time livelihood, schools of ministry are able to hold costs down while providing targeted educations. Their flexible structures position them to be adaptable and responsive to a religious landscape that's rife with change.

More can be done, however, to encourage laypeople to tap resources at schools of ministry, traditional seminaries, and other institutions. Current certificate programs are still dominated by the professional model. We need more types of certificates to be offered in areas such as preaching, evangelism, adult Christian education, and pastoral care. We also need more congregations to incentivize lay scholarship by committing to have skin in the game. A local church might start by paying for some or all of the course work, but just as important: The church could commit to providing a stipend for someone who's pursued some expertise. Although laypeople don't need a certificate to preach in the UCC, for instance, a congregation might agree to pay a reasonable fee for those who get appropriately trained and obtain a certificate. They might designate an evangelist, too. They might compensate monthly this person who gets an evangelism certificate and puts the knowledge to work by evangelizing and by teaching others in the congregation to do likewise.

This type of compensation structure, involving modest fees that might only be enough to cover a household's electric bill, could be nonetheless controversial in some church cultures. Concerns about motives could crop up as faith communities ask: shouldn't evangelists and lay preachers be motivated only by love of Jesus and passion for sharing the gospel? One might say yes, but if they're not cultivating skills to witness as well as possible, then perhaps further incentive is needed just to compensate them for time they invest along the way. After all, full-time pastors are compensated for whatever they do as part of their forty-plus hours in ministry each week, whether that involves sermon preparation, evangelism, pastoral care, denominational meetings, or other tasks. When the tasks are divvied up among congregants and part-time clerics, then it could make sense—at least in some ministry settings—to incentivize the cultivation of proficiencies among those of every status who love God but can't afford to donate lots of time to the church.

This renaissance in lay theological education could endow the church with more than a small army of strategically equipped individuals. It could also offer a less tangible but no less urgent benefit: robust ecclesiology in the pews. In my experience, laypeople often see the church as an institution to be maintained and a community of friends with a shared history. When responsibility for claiming a higher, holy mission is projected onto the pastor alone, the people don't take ownership of the church's eternal mission as a divinely inspired witness and a unique vessel of grace. Some even reduce it to a business that just needs to cover its nut and generate a surplus each year in order to be successful. This is somewhat understandable given their backgrounds as businesspeople and given the church's longstanding position that laypeople don't need advanced theological education; only pastors do. But this state of affairs need not saddle the church forever with an artificially small, inaccurate understanding of herself or her mission. When congregations invest in theological training for even one or two laypeople, they break the veil such that the pastor is no longer set apart as the only one bringing a bigger vision to bear. Our institutions of higher theological education can help laypeople appreciate the church's higher calling, see how it's rooted in God's design, and let it inform the organizational restructuring that so often accompanies shifts to part-time clergy.

CLERGY TRAINING: KEEP COSTS DOWN

Even as laypeople come to access theological education more routinely, the mission to train clergy remains a pillar—and one that needs updating if congregations are to get the part-time clergy they need. Tomorrow's clergy can't be as saddled with stress and debt as today's clergy are. The financial strain is bad for morale and hastens the departure of clergy from parish ministry. Making clergy education much more affordable is crucial for those on the path to part-time ministry. Emerging models are showing what's possible and worth replicating.

The Episcopal Diocese of Texas realized it had struck a chord when a newly founded school for future part-time priests began attracting distance-learning students from around the country. Established in 2004, the Iona School of Ministry was created initially to help small East Texas congregations that couldn't afford a full-time priest and couldn't attract qualified part-timers to serve. Solution: turn laypeople into priests who will remain local and serve their home congregations while keeping their day jobs in whichever fields they happen to work. The model would gather postulants in clusters to watch taped lectures from professors at the Seminary of the Southwest, an Episcopal seminary in Austin, and discuss what they've been hearing and reading with guidance from qualified facilitators. Retreats and other experiences are part of the program, but all is tailored to work within manageable parameters for people with children at home, full-time jobs, and other types of ongoing responsibilities. The three-year program for priesthood training costs $2,600 per year for students from the Diocese of Texas, which subsidizes the cost of educating them. For students from other dioceses, the cost is $4,000 per year.[5] That marks a dramatic savings over what's offered through ATS schools, where the average annual tuition and fees for MDiv students runs about $15,000 in programs enrolling 150 or fewer, which is the majority of ATS programs.[6] No wonder students have enrolled from at least seven other dioceses, including some as far away as Wyoming and New Hampshire. After graduating, they can be ordained and serve without the financial strain that burdens clerics who took out substantial loans and ended up unwittingly in part-time ministry positions. The success of the Iona program has allowed it to expand into offering just the types of tracks that laypeople in part-time congregations need: lay preacher, worship leader, catechist, and evangelist roles. The partnership between the traditional seminary and the diocese marks a good example of taking steps to identify assets (i.e., theological education resources) and repurpose them to be accessible and affordable in settings where they're needed. If this type of project were replicated in other denominations, part-time congregations would be better equipped to thrive.

Online learning must also continue its trajectory as an ever more viable way to get an ordination-track theological education. Online-only degree programs are now offered through about seventy of the 270-plus graduate schools accredited by ATS. Like other distance learning models, they would ideally be augmented by face-to-face interactions for the sake of spiritual formation in community. But that shouldn't give pause to the other 75 percent of ATS schools that still don't offer online degrees. They're now competing with online programs from brick-and-mortar schools that offer higher-cost master of divinity degrees. These cost and convenience factors are too important to ignore. Financial pitfalls have become such a problem that sixty-seven ATS schools have for a decade been tackling the problem with an Economic Challenges Facing Future Ministers initiative that aims to boost financial literacy and reduce unmanageable debt.[7] In this environment, schools need to throw tomorrow's clergy a lifeline that would let them enter ordained ministry responsibly. How online options get fine-tuned will be for educators to parse, but the sooner they work it out, the better for congregations with part-time clergy.

A third pathway to ordination has been gaining traction and warrants scaling up: customized learning. In these systems, a layperson discerning a call to ministry works with judicatory authorities to come up with a program that builds uniquely on what she already knows. Someone with an associate degree from a Bible college or a bachelor of arts in religious studies won't need the same Bible basics as a person with no such background. Advanced training in areas such as history and counseling can be leveraged, too, until it's clear exactly which gaps the candidate needs to fill academically and via field work.

Episcopal dioceses are finding this model meets the needs of a diverse set of dioceses where part-time pastorates have become commonplace. Episcopalians are using them, for instance, in the Diocese of Vermont, where small rural congregations are the norm and the majority have no full-time clergy. Tiny Christ Church in Bethel has raised up a second priest through this channel and a third is currently in training. When this latest one is ordained, this congregation of twenty will have three home-grown, elsewhere-employed, part-time priests taking turns at the altar and making sure no one gets burned out. Far from the rolling hills of New England, in metropolitan Pittsburgh, this training model for the priesthood has proven equally viable. It's used regularly in the Diocese of Pittsburgh, where three-quarters of congregations have no full-time priest. Their best bet to find a high-quality priest, they've learned, is to pluck someone with the right attributes from their own pews and develop him in a custom path approved by the bishop and commission on ministry.

As much as the above education models vary, they provide a strong basis for hope that the ranks of part-time clergy will not be starved for either intellectual or spiritual formation. Mainline denominations have inherited riches in theological education, albeit sometimes trapped in costly and hard-to-access packages. What these initiatives show is the degree to which these assets can be released and redeployed in ways that meet today's needs. Our traditions of relying on educated clergy will neither disappear nor be compromised if we learn to engage our inheritance with this type of open creativity.

TRAINING LEADERS FOR PART-TIME CONTEXTS

Theological schools must begin helping tomorrow's church leaders recognize how part-time congregations function within a distinct context. Schools can make sure pastors know how to discern with their congregants which part-time pastorate model is the best fit. Pastors also need to know how a conceptual model becomes a working reality in a particular congregation and when and how to tweak it over time. The art of getting the part-time model right is a new one for many mainline congregations and learning how to do it will be time well spent.

Church leaders in training need to begin broadly by letting their minds be stretched. Hued by the full-time bias, many will bring part-time ministry stereotypes that need to be unlearned. They'll need to stop thinking of part-time as synonymous with half-assed or half-dead. Isaiah 43:19, "I am about to do a new thing; . . . do you not perceive it?" could be the tagline verse for this part of their educations.

Instructors will need to guide leaders-in-training to reflect upon what it means that the pastorate won't be theirs alone to administer but shared among the many who have also been gifted by the Holy Spirit (1 Cor. 12). This can involve introducing part-time ministry models that facilitate thriving, such as the ambassador, equipper, and multi-staff-team-member models from chapter 3. In an educational environment, where imaginations can run wild, students can creatively theorize which part-time pastorate model belongs in which type of congregational setting. They might be tasked to get out in the field and exegete congregational settings. They might assess which model(s) they determine to be at work and which they might prescribe instead or in addition. In the process, they might identify more models beyond the three discussed in this book and lift them up for others to adopt. In a world where nearly half of all mainline congregations have no full-time paid clergy, every pastor-in-training needs to come to grips with what makes part-time churches inherently different. Even those who never end up serving part-time need to know what makes these sister churches tick; they can be strategically supportive if they understand what's going on inside. Such "outsiders" can sometimes offer the wisest counsel if they know what it is that they're seeing and what it says about the dynamics at play.

Pastors who are taught to think strategically about models will have a running start when they arrive in settings that need effective part-time ministry. This mental habit involves knowing how to spot assets that can be deployed— and not necessarily in the way they're deployed already. This technique of asset mapping is taught in Maine, where two-thirds of UCC congregations have no full-time clergy. The Maine Conference of the UCC has learned, after multiple generations of nurturing part-time churches, that asset mapping works.[8] Congregations learn to see abundance at their disposal, which leads to the next strategic move that pastors need to learn: leveraging. How might that storage room full of unused clutter be leveraged for mission, say, by storing food pantry goods or giving kids a place to study after school? Strategic thinking involves planning ahead for how resources of all types (spiritual, material, time) will be deployed in pursuit of particular types of outcomes that align with a congregation's highest values and priorities. The flipside involves learning to shed burdensome baggage of all types (emotional, material) that weighs down a faith community, prevents it from being nimble and keeps mission impacts mediocre. That's how Tuttle Road United Methodist Church in Cumberland, Maine, managed to add impactful new outreach ministries without overburdening its already-dedicated volunteers. The Rev. Linda Brewster guided the congregation in a process of identifying which legacy ministries no longer warranted sustaining because the church wasn't showing enough heart for them. Clergy need to learn how to help their congregations think in that type of strategic manner. Getting to that point should be part of their theological educations.

Clergy also need to be able to interpret what God is doing before their eyes when a congregation begins to experience new life or a renewed identity after going part-time. For instance, in Arlington, Virginia, Clarendon Presbyterian Church began rethinking a lot more than its pastor's job description. Many are used to unconventional thinking in this congregation where entrepreneurs, immigrants, and gay men with artistic backgrounds are well-represented and shepherded by a pastor whose intellectual curiosity netted him four advanced degrees along the way. Worship space got a makeover as pews came out and attractive, portable, comfortable seating came in. Congregants immediately found their Sunday assembly wasn't dwarfed by its space anymore. The permanent furniture no longer forced congregants into a feeling of: "Oh no, we have empty pews! We must be doing church wrong!" By taking control of how the space is furnished each week, Clarendon is able to foster intimacy and hospitality by putting out just enough seating to feel cozy and still have spots available for unexpected guests. This evolved with guidance from Pastor David Ensign, who helped the congregation own the idea that it's OK to be their size and to be playfully flexible in ways that they couldn't be decades ago.

With a resized pastorate, a reconfigured staff, and a reappointed sanctuary, Clarendon was on a roll and did not stop. The congregation remade its music ministry via the difficult but validated decision to bring in a new pianist with a new approach. Gone now was the uniformly classic hymnody that had marked the sound of worship at Clarendon for many years. In came a vibrant, fresh, and bubbly new sound when a pianist known for livening up Sunday brunch at Washington-area restaurants took the musical reins. Ensign gently guided the transformation by assuring laypeople they could think in fresh new ways and not betray church tradition. As an artist with a talent for reading cultural cues, Ensign had identified that his faith community was coming out of its cocoon. It was no longer afraid to leave behind the trappings of "church as it should be" with a full-time pastorate, wooden pews, traditional music, and other trappings of recent decades. Together with his session, Ensign helped to channel the congregation's sense of calling to become something quirkier, more avant-garde and playful. Living into this identity has joyfully been part of embracing not only a downsized pastorate but also the identity that has flowed from this transition.

Other congregations can also have similarly well-shepherded experiences, even if they move grudgingly into a part-time structure. But whether they do should not depend solely on whether they are blessed to have a pastor like Brewster or Ensign, that is, someone who knows perhaps instinctively how to lead a strategic reassessment of a congregation's assets. Pastors-in-training, as well as pastors in continuing education, can learn the art of leading these types of processes gently and encouragingly in congregations that are nervous about the shift to part-time. In that they can learn to usher in the new thing that God is doing, even if not everyone sees it.

TEACH DISCERNMENT

The part-timer has a particularly compelling need to spot underutilized spiritual gifts and help congregants do likewise. Blessings that might be taken for granted elsewhere can't be neglected or squandered in their settings. In settings where resources are contracting, every gift is too valuable to overlook.

But traditional theological education doesn't teach future clergy to spot and encourage pastoral gifts in the pews because, well, those are the pastor's domain. Or at least they used to be when full-time clergy were the dominant norm. Training instead focuses on preparing future pastors to do countless tasks *for* a congregation in areas from administration to oration and counseling. If congregants have gifts in those areas or others where the full-time pastor is paid to be proficient, then those gifts are likely to wither on the vine. Pastors haven't been taught or encouraged to notice them.

Theological schools can no longer leave the art of discernment to chance. They need to make sure students learn to spot where the Holy Spirit has left a mark on a parishioner's purpose, or where the Spirit continues to stir within the congregation. This could involve studying manifestations of the Holy Spirit in the Acts of the Apostles and learning to spot them in congregational life. Students might also learn how to listen to their intuitions, which can help them identify what's not being said explicitly but is being communicated, perhaps as unfulfilled yearnings and latent capacities among the flock. Guiding students into the discernment world of early church matriarchs and patriarchs, including the Egyptian desert mothers and fathers, could provide yet another way of exposing future clergy to an art form worthy of their mastery. When discernment is elevated to prominence among pastoral subjects taught in theological schools, a much-needed pillar to support part-time ministry will be going up.

Students learning to practice discernment could benefit from field work in part-time congregations that carve out space for it. In my congregation, the practice doesn't involve sitting around and listening for a still, small voice— or a loud, barking one for that matter. We make room for discernment by giving parishioners encouragement and space to experiment and try out new roles. In this, they're supported to set aside the inner Martha, which gets a lot of exercise in keeping up with a small church's chores, and let the inner Mary come out. We have, for example, an effective lay leader who had had enough of organizing Congregationalists (a task that can resemble herding cats) and became less active in church as months passed. A turning point came when the board of deacons made space for her to spread her wings in a new way as an instrumentalist at a special evening worship service. The moment was significant because although she'd played in church on occasion, she'd never been given top billing as the anchor musician. She'd been invited to shine because the deacons discerned that she had a gift waiting to be exercised and shared in a bigger way.

She readily accepted, practiced diligently to prepare, and delighted in offering her creative side to God in corporate worship. More flourishing followed. She started accompanying deacons monthly to visit parishioners at a nursing home. There she plays her instrument, a lovely string autoharp, while residents receive Communion. That led to a volunteer gig of sorts at our food pantry, where a retired church musician plays hymns and other songs on piano while guests "shop" for week's supplies. Now our parishioner steps in when the pianist goes on break. Her autoharp fills the sanctuary with a relaxing vibe and a tranquil beauty. A retiree herself, she has found a way to deliver a soulful blessing from a part of her that had not yet blossomed when her substantial skills as a lay leader were in high demand.

Knowing when to invite and how to expand the stage for a burgeoning outreach musician have been marks of discernment in action among the deacons at First Parish Church of Newbury. Clergy can learn to work similarly by making room for what needs to come out and nurturing it along—whether that's an individual calling, a short-term initiative, or the congregation's awareness of its true mission.

DEVELOPING SKILLS FOR MINISTRY MODELS

In vital congregations with part-time clergy, pastors are exercising specific skills that nobody taught them in mainline seminaries. Through a combination of personal gifts, promising local conditions, and movement of the Holy Spirit, they've witnessed more vitality than anyone thought could come after a switch to part-time. The challenge now is to systematize what works. This will involve preparing tomorrow's part-time pastors not only to think in terms of models and strategies, but also to have the requisite skills in their ministry toolboxes such that they can pull out what's needed and put it to work. This would mean learning, whether in seminary or through another training path, to be what each model asks of the pastor.

For the equipping model, a pastor needs to learn pedagogy. At the heart of the model lie three assumptions: the pastor is competent in several ministry areas, congregants are willing to learn those ministry arts, and the pastor is capable to teach them. For this last assumption to hold up, theological educators need to include pedagogy so that tomorrow's pastors have skills to teach what they know. Being able to give a great sermon is not the same as being able to teach someone else to do likewise. In fact, pastors are traditionally trained to do what others cannot do in the church and provide these functions for them as a service. That philosophy is no longer tenable, as we've seen, yet clergy-in-training aren't learning to build up others to do the very ministries they themselves do. Here we're talking about teaching one parishioner or small group how to deliver a homily, lead a small group, introduce the faith to the curious, and so forth. By learning basic pedagogical theory and discovering methods for various learning styles, clergy won't feel in over their heads. They'll be able step into any setting that is poised to thrive with a part-time pastor as long as he understands how to deploy the equipping model. Dispatching an army of pastors with that capacity would position scores of part-time churches to bear faithful witness and thrive.

Congregations that strategically leverage their pastor's time to make her an ambassador in the community need a pastor who knows how to be such a presence. An ambassador becomes a vicar of Christ and his church, and while every pastor plays such a role, the ambassador model requires a strategically informed intentionality. One needs to respond with grace when someone in the general public is skeptical, hostile, curious, or otherwise disposed. The ambassador needs a deep understanding of evangelism:

how it entails building relationships, not just getting people to worship on Sundays or utter rote phrases. The importance of being a capable, authentic communicator on the internet cannot be overstated for the ambassador, whose cyber-presence commands a potent influence in its own right. Clergy-in-training need to study practitioners of the model, try their hand at various techniques, and learn to listen just as well as they testify. This type of education attends to what it means to be a pastor today and to exercise pastoral authority in a community that might not think much of pastors, but nonetheless expects a church to be represented publicly by one. The ambassador pastor must learn to leverage both the office and the wider culture's view of that office as a representation of the church in a decidedly non-Christian world. The more the pastor knows about the dynamics at work, the more he can use this clout effectively.

Pastors need to hone skills in a third area, collaboration, if they're going to be well-positioned to contribute on an increasingly part-time landscape. Though working with others is no foreign task to any clergyperson, today's organizational environment is "flatter," less hierarchical, than many were taught to expect when they were groomed for full-time roles. A part-time pastor needs to know how to get accountability for a shared vision even when she doesn't have the capacity to constantly monitor or manage the execution. In a multi-staff model, this cleric also needs to work with a governing board to design other part-time staff positions to ensure strategic compatibility with the pastor's duties, gifts, and passions. The part-time pastor in this model must be a systemic thinker who can see how numerous pieces ought to fit together, and also how they can be fruitfully adjusted when they don't mesh as planned. The role involves constantly analyzing how the congregation can make the most of a few carefully positioned specialists on the staff. Another dimension calls for orchestrating missional partnerships with other organizations. These can amplify a part-time congregation's contributions to its community, but only if a congregation can chart a realistic course in light of its nontraditional staffing structure and limited capacity for execution. With so many moving pieces delicately aligned, the multi-staff terrain is rife with potential pitfalls. Yet it's also ripe with opportunity for congregations with leaders who can deliver on it. Prospects for success will be much enhanced by education that removes a lot of the guesswork and gives leaders the know-how they'll need.

EDUCATING PASTORS FOR NONCHURCH WORK

Visionary institutions could go one step further by facilitating side-career pathways for tomorrow's part-time clergy to follow. This approach would add a third way beyond today's two most prominent models, which either (1) train a person for full-time ministry or (2) equip a second-career mid-lifer/retiree to add ministry to an already-rich repertoire of personal and work experience. The third way would form them both for part-time ministry and for another line of work. Such institutions might partner, for instance, with trade schools. Enrollees would get their theological training while also pursuing a trade track such as carpentry, coding, or website design. They would graduate ready to ply their trades either full-time or part-time and lead a mainline congregation, too.

One might ask: why would anyone interested in a trade career bother to get trained in ministry? Because God still calls people to ministry, just not always as a full-time career. Young adults still feel called to ministry, but their generation has a strong pragmatic streak. They won't borrow heavily to launch a career that doesn't make economic sense. What's more, those drawn to the trades are not one-dimensional people. Many crave to use another side of their brains or use another part of themselves that doesn't get much chance to blossom in the workplace or in the home. Some can find their richest opportunity to do that as part-time clergy, but they also need sufficient income. That's why they would pursue both together as a matter of preparation—not just for a livelihood, but for a life enriched by complementary opportunities to grow as the multifaceted creature that God created.

Chapter 6

TEAMING UP

Leveraging Partnerships
Is a Part-Time Church's Sweet Spot

The first time I reflected publicly on the role part-time ministry plays in my life, listeners reacted with a lot more surprise and excitement than I'd expected. Having come to Portland, Maine, for a conference on part-time ministry in April 2018, they brought plenty of their own experience as part-time pastors and parishioners. Why should my story be eye-opening for these veterans?

It turns out they'd never thought about part-time ministry as I was framing it—rich with advantages that full-time ministry doesn't afford for people with a creative bent, including writers like myself. These churchmen and churchwomen had been used to seeing part-time ministry as an unfortunate fact of life that must just be accepted, like death, taxes, and traffic jams. They were used to lamenting: if only every church could afford a full-time pastor, then all Christendom would be better off. But in my talk, they heard how the part-time aspect of the pastorate has enriched my life. It got them wondering: if it has worked that way for me, then maybe it could—and often does—work that way in the lives of other clergypersons. Rather than limit possibilities, part-time can be the perfect ticket to expanding them.

I told them how part-time ministry has functioned as a grounding anchor in my life. Part of that anchoring has been spiritual, manifest in vocational disciplines. As a weekly preacher, I pivot from chasing news sources and digesting feedback from editors to doing what it takes to prepare a sermon. With a deep breath, I study and pray with the Bible. I poke through concordances and commentaries for deeper insights. Then I walk along the ocean with the faces of my congregation in my mind's eye, cooking up illustrations that might hold their attention or soften up their hearts, even for a few seconds. The practice drags me out of my self-centered ruminations, forcing me to ponder God's grace and mercy as I go about my life as a journalist, a neighbor, and a family member. The habit leavens the loaf of whatever I happen to be baking that week. It betters me.

But it was a different type of anchoring that really surprised the Maine crowd. I told them how part-time ministry also grounds me financially. Knowing I live in the expensive Greater Boston area, they wondered how part-time pay could possibly be stabilizing—or anything but frustrating for that matter. I explained that for us freelance writers, as for many other self-employed artists and craftspeople, having one solid part-time gig with a steady paycheck can be enough to stabilize, even catalyze, a creative career for years or decades. Monthly variability in self-employed income becomes far more manageable when one client (in my case, the church) provides a reliable cash flow. That would seem like personal finance wonkery except it represents much more. It allows me to take risks and use my craft for a greater good than just remuneration. I've said yes, for instance, to low-paying clients who want stories about revitalizing Sunday school, or about challenges facing kids who have an incarcerated parent. These bring an element of risk for writers because we don't know how long they'll take to execute, and if they don't pay much, then we could find ourselves in a jam if the research drags on. But I can accept meaningful assignments while some of my writer friends find they can work only for the highest bidders. They complain about feeling like sellouts, doing work that doesn't resonate with why they became writers in the first place. I am blessed not to have that problem. I can dedicate large chunks of my production each year to reporting important news that is underreported in the media and that certainly will not get covered unless I do it myself. That's because other reporters either aren't interested in these topics or aren't able to commit the time. All this is possible because a church's financial resources are no longer captive to a mission of paying 100 percent of one professional's salary and benefits. They can now be the financial basis for a creative contractor's career that includes contributions in and far beyond the church.

My experience offers a window into the beautiful new thing God is doing, often secretly, as clergy staffing is downsized in mainline Protestant congregations. A garden is springing up in the vacuum left by the departure of the full-time, professional cleric. Pastors are finding there's no need to abandon other professional, artistic, or activist interests. We can keep at them while keeping a hand in ministry. We can do it by serving congregations that aren't as rich as they used to be, yet still have the wherewithal to recover a beneficent tradition: the church as benefactor of the arts. When a church provides enough income to give a creative cleric a running start financially each month, it relieves much of the pressure and is in effect commissioning his art. Though the church officially compensates only for work done on behalf of the church, it is also enabling a way of life by limiting how much time is expected for ministry and freeing up the part-time pastor to serve the world in other ways. That's what being an ecclesiastical benefactor of the arts looks like for most of mainline Protestantism in the twenty-first century. One won't find artists being sponsored in congregations with full-time clergy, whose compensation packages consume a large chunk of the annual budget but leave the cleric no substantial time for creative pursuits. Today's underwriting of the arts comes instead from congregations with part-time clergy, who receive not only a financial boost but also the commodity of greatest value to an artist: time. We get time away from parish responsibilities to draw, build, paint, dance, make films, play an instrument—whatever the vocation might be. God is enabling our churches to bless the world with beautiful, thought-provoking, significant art once again.

This mode of indirectly supporting a myriad of clergy ventures beyond the church world brings the right dynamics to bear at just the right time to enhance vitality in part-time congregations. That's because the universe of potential partners has never been larger. In America, 56.7 million people including myself work as freelancers.[1] We are self-employed, just like independent attorneys, chiropractors, or carpenters who hang out a shingle saying, "open for business." We work directly for clients, and our ranks are growing rapidly because companies want the flexibility that comes with having contractors, not employees. By 2027, the majority of American workers will be freelancers.[2] Although some freelance out of necessity and would prefer full-time employment, the majority increasingly does it because workers value the flexibility and freedom.[3] This workforce environment is great news for congregations with part-time clergy. It means their clerics will likely come from the growing ranks of skilled people who now have an art, craft, or trade that they practice independently. Churches will need these types of clerics, who bring to the table a capacity for supporting themselves financially. And part-time churches will bring a strong proposition of their own as they offer prospective clergy a meaningful endeavor to live out their calling with compensation and without a full-time commitment. Congregations with part-time clergy are in effect clients of the freelance economy. In an economic sense, they are putting freelance clergy on retainer, often indefinitely, for ten, twenty, or thirty hours a week. What better time to offer such arrangements than when the workforce is nearing a freelance majority and mainline Protestant congregations are fast converting their pulpits to part-time. In the American way of work, what's happening in the larger culture and what's occurring in the church could not be more perfectly aligned.

Pastors are already structuring their lives to take advantage of new opportunities and contribute on the levels that churches need. In Carlsbad, New Mexico, Pastor David Rogers works as an adjunct professor, a hospice chaplain, and a commercial kitchen supervisor at an addiction rehabilitation facility. Pastor David Ensign writes songs, poetry, stories, and documentary film scripts during his time off from Clarendon Presbyterian. At the Maine conference in 2018, I met an electrician, a filmmaker, an adjunct lecturer, and a social worker in an urban prison system—all serving local congregations as part-time clergy. None were working in ministry because they had to. We were seeing the tip of the iceberg in terms of the new ways in which congregations are making rich lives and self-employed livelihoods possible for their pastors.

But clergy aren't the only ones discovering a new world of opportunity in this unsung corner of the religious landscape. Laypeople find that in the absence of full-time clergy presence, they discover outlets for expressing creative talents that haven't yet flourished in community. Earlier in this book, we looked at how laity are responding to pastoral needs by filling voids, often in joyful and fulfilling ways. However, the vacuum that's opened up with the departure of full-time clergy also allows laypeople to spread wings and flourish in creative ways. They find more opportunities to take initiative, organize events, and spearhead programs that wouldn't happen under a full-time pastorate where such things are thought to be the pastor's job—or at least require the pastor's blessing, which significantly narrows what's possible. In a part-time setting, the pastor is not around all week to hover or check up on all that's happening at the church. As laypeople get used to these conditions, they go from lamenting the absence of constant pastoral direction and oversight to relishing the freedom and flexibility. This ushers in waves of creativity that suggest something profound is happening. The church is becoming a space where people can imagine, dabble, and create within safe parameters. It resembles a former mill building that was underutilized for a time but is now hospitable to micro-manufacturers, artists, and artisans. The congregation brings much to the table in terms of history, stature, location, and mission. But in the absence of full-time clergy staff, its need for community partners to help develop latent assets is clearer and more compelling than in full-time congregations where partnering is optional. Partners of all types see opportunities to help the part-time church become what it otherwise could not. As long as the church remains clear about its mission and values, wisely discerned partnerships can help a congregation deliver on its not-yet-fulfilled promise.

With conditions ripe for congregations with part-time clergy to host and fuel a new wave of church-based creativity, radars need to be alert for partnership opportunities. Part-time congregations are built for partnerships because they have infrastructure galore to offer and they can't maximize their assets by themselves. In the new absence of full-time clergy, well-conceived partnerships can ensure opportunity with accountability and prevent the quiet languishing that can occur when congregations simply fail to act. The latter scenario of inactivity too often plays out when a congregation isn't thoughtful about taking control and repurposing infrastructure because, quite simply, the pastor used to run the show and now they don't know where to begin. Thoughtful partnering to encourage artistic flourishing in and alongside congregational life is a marvelous place to begin, especially because risks can be minimized without much trouble.

GOT NICE SPACE? USE IT FOR ART SHOWS

Congregations can boost the energy and "buzz" in their communities by offering local artists something that churches have in spades: attractive space. Across the country, hundreds of congregations have over the past decade either added or expanded art galleries.[4] The idea: turn underutilized wall space in hallways, narthexes, and fellowship halls into exhibit areas for local artists. The trend has caught on to the degree that more than 400 congregations paid $30 each for a copy of a church gallery launch guide from the nonprofit Christians in the Visual Arts. How mainline Protestant churches set up their galleries can vary widely. At First Presbyterian Church in Fort Wayne, Indiana, gallery space is used to showcase works by secular artists and facilitate dialogue between religious and secular communities that normally wouldn't reflect together on profound questions. At Bethlehem Lutheran Church in Minnetonka, Minnesota, Pastor James Disney seeks out contributors to thematic shows that dovetail with liturgical seasons. In 2017, an Easter show featured works in the vein of an ode to joyful music.

"When we have receptions for the artists, they invite their friends and co-workers and people they met at the grocery store," Disney said. "We get a lot of remarks about, 'How amazing that you're doing this! Wow, this is incredible!' It sort of reshapes their vision about what church is about."

Galleries are increasingly found in all kinds of churches, from evangelical megachurches to small mainline congregations, as leaders recognize the many possibilities and limited downsides. Lincoln Berean Church in Lincoln, Nebraska, once proudly displayed quilts lovingly made by forty church members. Another Lincoln Berean show used photos to give the city's many tattooed residents a chance to tell church folk what their tattoos mean to them. Venues can be created anywhere underutilized space cries out in a fellowship hall, hallway, narthex, or somewhere else. Turning such space into an exhibit area can be as inexpensive as putting up a few hooks and thin wires. Even the most high-end installations with tasteful track lighting and other adornments don't need to cost more than

$1,000, according to CIVA. Once the galleries are created, congregations can stage receptions that bring neighbors and art lovers into the church for the first time. They can help local artists get visibility without having to pay hefty commissions to art dealers. They can design shows around any themes they want, from seasonal and theological subjects to broadly spiritual issues like trauma, oppression, healing, and love. As long as they're clear about guidelines and don't allow obscene or otherwise inappropriate displays, churches run minimal risks. And they have much to gain by convening the religious and non-religious around visuals that transcend language in a time when words are so often divisive.

For congregations with part-time clergy, hosting galleries marks just one of many promising ways to partner with artistic groups and create win-win opportunities. Such churches have much to offer both in the form of beautiful, often underutilized physical spaces and in their weekly gathering practices. Broadly construed, Christian worship brings people together for praising God by pointing God's people upward to what is good, right, and true. Why not find room in sanctuaries and in worship services for artists to help point the people upward? Maybe create space within liturgies for artists to let their works function as icons in complementing prayer or facilitating testimonies. Of course, some traditions would flinch at the idea of images in worship for reasons dating back to the Reformation, but many mainliners have relaxed their sensitivities to such things. Letting art flourish anew as an elixir for the soul can become a niche where congregations with part-time clergy soar, get noticed, and impact their communities by leveraging the power of partnerships.

BREAK A LEG: TEAMING UP
WITH THEATER TYPES

Congregations and theater groups make for natural allies. They can be especially helpful to each other when clergy are serving part-time.

In theater, nineteenth-century Danish theologian Søren Kierkegaard found a metaphor that has shaped mainline Protestant understandings ever since. "God is the critical theatergoer," Kierkegaard writes, "who looks on to see how the lines are spoken and how they are listened to: hence here the customary audience is wanting. The speaker is then the prompter, and the listener stands openly before God."[5] This theatrical aspect is palpable every Sunday in dramatic elements of instrumental music, singing, public readings, sometimes even dance. Because these worlds share so much overlapping terrain, the congregation with part-time clergy is apt to find a key partner in its local theater group.

Like visual artists, thespians can take advantage of underutilized spaces that are already set up for an audience. Churches that offer space for rehearsals and performances stand poised to build lasting relationships with locals who love a good public drama. Such relationships can begin promisingly with a good-will gesture from the church. Even the most cash-strapped congregation can show largesse because it has so much to offer, including a unique space in town and the stature that comes with being a local religious institution. Sharing from those wellsprings doesn't need to cost the church much money, if any. In some settings, charging rent might be appropriate. Either way, it can confer game-changing benefits to a theater group that doesn't have its own space or needs a unique space for a special occasion. These steps can seed new relationships with neighbors who believe in gatherings, in insightful depictions, in uplift, and in heightened awareness. These are people who get, on some level, what church is about. Connecting on that level will lay a foundation for building relationships.

A congregation with part-time clergy can assertively explain to its theatrical guests how this isn't an ordinary church. Nor are its opportunities ordinary for those with acting, directing, or musical talent. If you have abilities and want to try out working in a new genre, for instance, the congregation can work with you to make it happen in a worshipful, Christian context. The faithful need a liaison, who doesn't have to be the pastor (although it could be), to articulate for theatrical neighbors how a vast new world of artistic opportunity has opened up in this congregation as a result of the pastorate moving to part-time. Now the formats are more flexible. The invitation for lay leadership as well as lay participation in seasonal pageants, poignant skits, and allegorical presentations are more generous. This can come as a great surprise, for instance, to lapsed Christians who haven't been to church in years and might assume liturgical initiatives must originate with an authoritative clergy presence. Those who've never had a church background might be shocked to learn one doesn't need to be a dyed-in-the-wool believer in order to take part in worship or in Christian productions. That participants are on a spiritual journey, not finished products, is not well understood in creative communities that equate Christianity with a shrill, off-putting form of it that they've encountered and rejected. In an era marked by low religious literacy,[6] the general public too is apt to have little understanding of what's possible in terms of a drama within a faith community.

Targeted communication that unpacks opportunities for those who already embrace theatrical arts is a promising place to begin.

GIVE MUSICIANS A CHANCE

Skilled amateur musicians can find the best of all worlds in congregations led by part-time clergy. Consider that larger churches with full-time clergy tend to rely on professional players to deliver the polished sounds that worshipers in a consumer mode expect and sometimes even demand. Such settings aren't hospitable to the person who'll never be a pro but is progressively learning an instrument or keeping up her skills from childhood. A congregation with part-time clergy can be an artistic oasis for this person, whether she is eight, eighteen, or eighty-eight years old. The churches I've served have always been magnets for good amateur musicians, who weren't always committed believers but were eager to play guitar, dulcimer, or autoharp, sing solos, or otherwise contribute their gifts as offerings to the community and to God. We find that as musicians get wind of such an opportunity—to play before a small, encouraging crowd without having to make a religious commitment—they set aside Sunday mornings and drive some distances to participate. Some seem to grow in faith while others might not, but those outcomes are beyond our control. Our vitality is enhanced when they've felt welcome enough to take part and keep coming back. That starts with them being aware of the opportunity that congregations with part-time clergy embody distinctly for musicians like them.

Watching amateur musicians flourish ranks among the great joys of part-time ministry at my church. Players familiar with the congregation have learned they just need to spot an opportunity, make a proposal, or just start doing something musical and the sky is suddenly their limit. At our food pantry, for instance, an octogenarian volunteer who worships at our church in the summer realized that we have all these people around waiting for food and no one playing the piano. She made it her ministry to play for an hour each week, mixing hymns and familiar oldies to create a festive, spiritual atmosphere. Meanwhile, the lay leader-turned-musician I mentioned in chapter 5 started bringing her autoharp to play when the pianist takes a break. The pantry guests love the treat of listening to relaxing live music, such that now no one is in a rush to leave. And other musicians in her family have leapt at opportunities as well. Her husband knows that whenever he wants to play autoharp and sing in worship, we are glad to have him. And her pianist son came into his own as a musician at the church as well. While a law student, he went from filling in occasionally to being a regular part of our Sunday worship. He grew to where he sang along to his anthem selections, which was something he had never done publicly until he gained the confidence by playing in our supportive and appreciative church. He now works as a lawyer, plays in a popular band and—like musicians from Elvis Presley to Aretha Franklin to Fats Domino—builds on the opportunities he was afforded in church. Congregations with part-time clergy are continuing the tradition of making room at the table for those who can play and just need a chance.

With a dollop of irony, congregations with the most to offer emerging musicians often do the least to promote the opportunities. When these churches make the common mistake of turning inward and directing pastors to focus on parishioners' needs, effective public communication tumbles off the radar of priorities. Congregations can do better by having a music liaison keep an ear to the ground. Identify unsung talent and carve out standing platforms where players can be plugged in, such as anthems and preludes on a particular Sunday of the month. Would a teenager who's become proficient at the piano be welcomed to play? Then dispatch the liaison to spread the word at local music programs where kids take lessons or play in bands. Youngsters who jump at the chance to play before a church audience are apt to bring a crowd of adoring family members with them to the worship service. What about a few middle-aged guys who get together for a weekly jam session just for fun? If they're good enough, would they be welcome to play a few worshipfully appropriate tunes as hymns or anthems? Then send the pastor or another ambassador to get acquainted, hear a recording, perhaps let them play on a Sunday morning. Results could be surprising as friends and family of amateur musicians come to worship and new relationships are born. A similar approach can make sense when hiring musicians, too. Church music consultant Kate Eaton urges congregations to look beyond church musician circles and tap players on their local gig scenes when seeking to liven up worship sounds because, as she told me, "we feel like they can bring another element of surprise."[7] Raising awareness of such opportunities, whether done in person or over the internet, is an art that any congregation can develop without much trouble. Those with part-time clergy just need to recognize the light of opportunity that lies in their midst and practice putting it on a stand for all to see.

Congregations can be creative in their own right and get a head start on new vitality by redirecting into music some of the dollars freed up by their transitions to part-time.

In Newport, Rhode Island, St. John the Evangelist Church does not utilize a part-time priest, but the church needed revitalizing after a period of conflict and used an innovative model that might work in certain settings that need a boost while adjusting to part-time. The congregation launched a professional children's choir.[8] Part of a choir school initiative with two other Newport-area churches, the young choristers are called "professional" because they get paid a modest $15 to $30 per month. That's enough, though, to teach them job responsibilities: attend rehearsals, sing twice a month in worship, and take part in special events such as Holy Week services. Parents pay $200 a year to have kids take part, and a trained choir director makes sure they're singing complex pieces at a high level. Congregational vitality gets a boost as worship attendance soars from twenty-five when the kids aren't singing to sixty when they are. Much of that includes the kids' family members and friends, who turn out to support them. Some had no church background but now are part of the congregation, saying they love the beauty of the Anglo-Catholic liturgy. Music grants help fund the program, which infuses the congregation with energy that wouldn't be there otherwise. The mission component blesses families with affordable music training for kids as young as seven. Such an initiative wouldn't work everywhere and might rub some purists the wrong way, but it makes worshipers out of many who wouldn't be there otherwise. And it's a model that could be adapted to fit whichever types of artistic training a church is prepared to offer.

With so much artistic experimentation afoot in part-time settings, the pastor's role includes making sure the faith focus doesn't get lost. For creativity to flourish, the congregation needs clear parameters from the pastor, who is still "lashed to the mast" and responsible for solid doctrine in worship. Encouraging creativity and extending a long leash doesn't mean anything goes, just as the long leash that denominations give part-time congregations doesn't mean they're sanctioned to wander from orthodox Christian teachings. The part-time pastor can play this shepherding role by reminding the flock, in sermons and open letters and elsewhere, of what the Christian faith proclaims to be truthful and good news. Though some might regard the idea of heresy as antiquated or laughable, part-time pastors need to be extra vigilant about avoiding it because they're the main (sometimes only) safeguards to make sure the congregation's Christian character and theology are preserved. When guiding participants on what's appropriate, pastors provide particular content for an artist to choose from or might otherwise set parameters to ensure a faithful witness comes through. This becomes especially important in a part-time setting, where creativity from the pews is strongly encouraged and guidance via denominational relationships isn't always robust. Mindful of these dynamics, the pastor needs to be like a host at a party or special function, graciously inviting all and clarifying a few helpful stipulations to ensure all can thrive at the event.

NATURAL TIES: TEAMING UP
FOR HUMAN SERVICES

Partnerships are not limited to artistic arenas. Congregations with part-time clergy can launch a wealth of mutually beneficial projects by teaming up with organizations that provide social services and education. The natural synergies cry out for collaboration. Local mainline churches tend to be long-established institutions with deep community relationships and unique physical infrastructure in prime locations for accessibility. Social service providers have skills in areas from nursing to social work, but aren't always trusted as much as the local church is. Schools always need volunteers, which even small congregations have, especially if they are at a vitality-enhancing stage of pivoting from being inwardly focused to being outwardly mission-oriented. These organizations can be as complementary as puzzle pieces en route to a common goal.

Free health clinics can put a congregation on the general public's radar while providing a much-needed service. Here part-time congregations can learn from their full-time counterparts who've had more staffing power to provide the initial organizing push—and consequently to see the benefits. For instance, St. Paul African Methodist Episcopal Church in Berkeley, California, has been offering blood pressure screenings since the 1990s and with increasing frequency in response to popular demand. Monthly diabetes screenings have been added, and the church's first cancer workshop drew a big crowd. The clinics make congregants more health-conscious, organizers say, and the congregation now takes pride in helping its African American neighborhood be healthier and better educated on matters of physical well-being. And part-timers with an entrepreneurial streak are finding health can be a draw that helps grow a church. For example, in Lewiston, Maine, a young Seventh Day Adventist congregation called Ark Fellowship has been growing inside a former Pizza Hut with help from the many health-related programs that happen during the week. For seven years, the Ark was anchored by the vegan Olive Branch Café, which transformed from a health-focused restaurant by day into a classroom space by night, offering free classes on topics from smoking cessation to reversing diabetes and plant-based cooking. Now the café is closed but the many health-related, educational ministries live on. Ark Fellowship worship services got their start with a carpenter who's also ordained. Participants in the Ark's various programs come from abutting neighborhoods where poverty and poorly managed health conditions have contributed to chronic despair and substance abuse. The congregation that meets there on Saturdays draws from the ranks of those who've been attending seminars, often led by experts in the region who donate their time, at The Ark during the week. These models keep costs to a minimum for congregations while delivering a meaningful blessing to communities and reawakening to the ancient link between faith and health.

School-based partnerships can be easy to launch and pack a powerful impact with no need for full-time clergy. Because congregations worry about separation of church and state, they don't always initiate working ties with schools, but unless they plan to proselytize (which mainline churches seldom do), such concerns are overblown. Churches can organize back-to-school drives that equip kids with basic school supplies such as backpacks, pencils, calculators, and notebooks. Afterschool programs like the one offered at New Sharon Congregational Church in New Sharon, Maine, can fill an important need. In Haw River, North Carolina, ninety-member St. Andrew's Episcopal Church is located next to a trailer park where most residents are Hispanic and not everyone speaks English. Through relationships with neighbors and local schools, the church learned that some kids probably wouldn't get help with homework unless the church provided it.

Volunteers now wait for kids to get home from school, run across the church lawn, and join people old enough to be their grandparents for snacks, followed by lessons in math and reading. That the vicar at St. Andrew's is part-time does not hamper the outreach. On the contrary, because members are accustomed to spearheading initiatives, the need they spotted turned into action quickly.

These types of partnerships rooted in human services keep a part-time congregation grounded and confident in its ability to make a meaningful difference in local people's lives. I have seen it in my congregation, which has scaled up its food pantry ministry to feed 150 or more in any given week. We do so in partnership with groups like Nourishing the North Shore, a nonprofit that gleans produce from fields of local farmers and makes it available to our pantry guests via a "free farmers market" that is a rarity among pantries. As joyful confidence grows among the faithful and communities are impacted for the better, the power of these partnerships speaks for itself.

COLLEGE CONNECTIONS

In reaching out to the world and introducing myriad opportunities that await artistic types, congregations need to make sure they don't overlook one key constituency: prospective part-time clergy. For several generations, whether or not to become clergy has been reduced to a career choice. Those with a spiritual bent or a heart for following Jesus have been asked in effect to discern: are you called to a be a full-time church professional who makes a living entirely from church work? This yes-or-no choice meant the church lost out on scores of potentially strong leaders with deep faith commitments and abundant gifts for the job only because they had more compelling professional interests. But now as thousands of congregations go part-time, the question of whether to become clergy and lead a parish can be entirely reframed. Now it's more akin to other questions that young adults consider, such as: whether to remain single, be coupled, cohabitate, or get married; whether or not to have children; whether to stay active in athletics, community service, or artistic pursuits; whether to live with aging parents; and so on. Being parish clergy in a mainline church is now something one can do alongside any of those things plus a full-time career in, say, science, business, government, or anything else. It can deliver a dimension of a rich, meaningful life, perhaps not for a lifetime but for a season when an individual has both the time and the proximity to a setting where he is needed as a pastor. The ministry can be spiritually rewarding and financially helpful to a degree, even if the dollars cover only some of a household's expenses. Denominations and congregations now need to raise awareness of this exciting form of clergy option for those discerning what to do as well-rounded people in young adulthood, in midlife adjustments, in empty-nester mode, or in retirement.

Connecting with high schools, trade schools, colleges, and graduate schools will advance this important outreach to future clergy. Such schools routinely host career fairs and panel presentations to familiarize students with paths they could pursue. Local pastors, bishops, and judicatory officers ought to have a presence at such events and deliver a voice for part-time opportunities. They should not be hesitant to visit public schools or other nonreligious institutions; explaining to students what clergy do is constitutional, legal, and appropriate in all types of schools.

What's more, their voices will inject a fresh energy and new perspective into events that otherwise get stale with the same voices being heard every year. Students with a church background or even a spiritual curiosity are apt to perk up and think: "Clergy? You mean I could get paid to be a pastor—and still be a bus driver, a wife, and a mom? Or I could work Sundays as a priest and during the week make my art or teach? Wow, I've never thought of that! What an amazing life that would be!"

Those who explain the part-time clergy option on campuses would be sought-after contacts for soon-to-be-graduates with a creative bent, a spiritual passion, and uncertainty about how to put it all together in a viable livelihood. After all, they're used to cobbling together multiple income streams. Many want the holy grail of work-life balance in the twenty-first century: flexibility with stability. The part-time clergy option could set off lightbulbs in young minds as the missing link they've been seeking as they navigate the freelance economy. Ministry could be the calling and job that brings just the right mix of meaning, creativity, flexibility, and security. Once their curiosity is piqued, all proper steps to decipher whether they're a fit for ordained or authorized ministry in a particular denomination can be pursued.

Those who question whether the church should be recruiting in such variegated contexts are likely trusting too much in antiquated assumptions. Denominations can no longer assume that those whom God has called to ministry will come to them. What life in the church has to offer for laypeople and clergy alike is poorly understood by today's college students, as mainline chaplains on college campuses roundly attested at a 2019 conference I attended. Churches need to be proactive in dispelling untruths and acquainting young people with how they could be valued. The risk of bringing in people who aren't truly committed to the church is low because denominational processes toward ordination are plenty demanding to weed out those who're just looking for a part-time job with weekend hours. We can trust our processes to vet those who are truly called, even when the initial pool is wider than in the past when gatekeepers spoke primarily with those potential candidates who came recommended by a pastor or other church leader. A wider pool can enable more of those with passion for Jesus and for building God's kingdom to find a place, however unlikely, within the leadership of the church. Their infusion will help mainline churches become less beholden to the sensibilities of individual families whose influence has at times become overdone, especially in local parish contexts where faith is largely transmitted only to those who share blood ties. Recruiting leaders from the general public, and not solely among the self-selected or from narrowly sectarian enclaves, will bring waves of new blood and energy that can only help fuel the vitality we see in pockets today.

CONCLUSION

This brings us back to where we started: recognizing the great, yet only slightly fulfilled promise of congregations with part-time clergy. We have seen how they can reverse decline by acting early, redistributing pastoral duties more evenly, and mobilizing outreach to people who crave the types of opportunities that are uniquely available in these settings. We have explored how denominations, educators, and creative partners can bring distinct muscle to bear in helping these congregations flourish to their potential. Now it's time for all these stakeholders to come together in positioning these congregations for a fresh act. They are like old sports cars found dust-covered and neglected behind a storage heap in a garage. They won't be faster than today's new models, but with a few tweaks and a little polish, they'll enjoy a new life as respected classics that can still motor. Preparing for their success means gearing them up for visibility, branding, and outreach. The rest will be up to God.

That congregations with part-time clergy must come out of the shadows and be counted is essential. As discussed above, they need a catchier label for their category, but that's not all. They also need to own the fact that they're a different kind of church with distinct experiences to offer. Currently, it's almost impossible to identify which denominational churches in a given area have part-time clergy. That's not because they're rare—they're not rare at all. It's because they hide their status as churches that use part-time clergy. Nothing on their websites, bulletins, or social media posts indicates that their clergy are not full-timers. These churches might not think such information is relevant to post, but more likely, they're ashamed. They might think part-time means the church is financially poor or has less to offer to a consumeristic world than a church with clergy on call 24/7. They're thinking in worldly, not godly, terms about wealth as being indicative of worth. We must break free from this trap. Just as many long-marginalized people are refusing to be shamed anymore for their disabilities or body types, congregations with part-time clergy need to be proudly acknowledged for who they are. They are like college athletic programs that might have competed in Division I at one time but evolved to fill a different niche, and now thrive

in Division II. This transition doesn't mean they've failed
or can't succeed in the years ahead. A D2 program can
produce superb athletes, mold character, and deliver hard-
won championships. With encouragement from powerful
allies around the church, these congregations likewise need
to step up and embrace their D2 moment. While it's true
they have fewer consumeristic perks to offer—no celebrity
guest speakers, no renowned musicians, no ten-week
programming with tidy handouts and curated activities
for every attendee—they absolutely offer experiences that
larger, full-time churches cannot touch. Being visible and
proudly part-time can be first steps toward fulfilling what
God has prepared for their new act.

Fresh branding will serve these congregations better
than a cool dip on a hot day. They need to lift up the types
of life-changing experiences that their people have had and
are still having, whether that's as artists who blossomed for
the first time or as lay ministers who became the hands and
feet of Christ in a new way. Learning to present themselves
effectively might involve working with judicatory staffers,
with consultants, or with local church members with relevant
storytelling skills. However they do it, these congregations
need to frame themselves as Christian communities where
people are made new through the special opportunities
and experiences they find there. Emphasize how being a
practitioner and builder (not a passive consumer) of a holy
community makes a meaningful difference. Be clear about
what's doable here that one wouldn't expect to find at a
typical church. Maybe call it a "flat church" (as opposed
to one that's rigidly siloed). Or call it a "priesthood-of-all-
believers church." Somehow, potential visitors should be
led to respond: "This isn't church as usual, or at least not
church as I've known it to be. It seems I could be me more

authentically, and maybe know God more honestly, at this church. I could try being and doing some new things that are really meaningful. I might need to check it out."

All this positioning means little if people don't get an invitation to experience what congregations with part-time clergy have to offer. All the pastorate models that we've seen garnering vitality in part-time congregations are freeing people up for effective outreach and evangelism. In the ambassador model, the pastor plays a special outreach role as a representative communicator, inviter, and liaison. In the equipper model, the pastor equips laypeople to do evangelism, increase hospitality, or otherwise make the outside world feel welcome. And in the multi-staff rubric, a member of the team can either be designated for direct outreach or coach laity in how to practice the art themselves. No matter who does it, the goals are the same. People unfamiliar with life in this congregation need to encounter someone who can speak from the heart about her experience of growing spiritually in this special setting. Perhaps someday congregations with part-time clergy will be organized to the point that they project a unified message on a wider platform. Then they might convey together how lives have been changed when the Holy Spirit moves in settings loosened up and repurposed by the arrival of part-time clergy. But until then, congregations need to take charge of telling their own stories and embodying what their communities stand for.

In Scripture, God loves to exceed the limits of what humans believe to be possible. We should not assume that God acts any differently today when the faithful are gathered. From the aged matriarchs who miraculously give birth to the sending of a humble and weaponless Savior, the Bible is consistent in promising that God will surprise and delight. Where some now see shrunken or static congregations and write them off as lost causes, God likely sees an underdog like the Hebrews of old: weak by worldly standards and therefore perfectly poised to reveal God's mighty power in surprising ways. Let's not discount these holy remnants too soon. Let's watch expectantly for new springs to break forth in the desert. Congregations with part-time clergy have been on the margins of church life for long enough. Their time at God's banquet is just beginning.

NOTES

INTRODUCTION

1. Quoted in Ellen Brown, "Writing Is Third Career for Morrison," Cincinnati Enquirer, Sept. 27, 1981, https://www.newspapers.com/clip/21863475/tonimorrison/.

2. "Congregational Vitality and Ministerial Excellence: Intersections and Possibilities for Ministry," by Kristina Lizardi-Hajbi for the United Church of Christ, June 2015.

CHAPTER 1: GOODBYE TO BIAS, STIGMA, AND IDOLS

1. Based on September 2016 analysis of 2014 and 2015 church data by Kirk Hadaway, former congregational research officer for the Episcopal Church. Spreadsheet was prepared for author at his request. The annual Episcopal Church Domestic Fast Facts report stopped publishing data on percentages of congregations with part-time clergy after 2014. The 2013–14 Domestic Fast Facts report is at https://www.episcopalchurch.org/files/documents/2014_fast_facts.pdf.

2. Based on author's analysis of statistics provided by major mainline denominations.

3. Congregations with full-time clergy here refers to those with pastors who work full-time in one local setting and

don't serve in other churches or work other jobs. Preliminary data from 2018–19 were provided to the author by National Congregations Study Director Mark Chaves.

4. "American Congregations 2015: Thriving and Surviving," Faith Communities Today, https://faithcommunitiestoday .org/wp-content/uploads/2019/01/American-Congregations -2015.pdf, 5.

5. Samuel L. Perry and Cyrus Schleifer, "Are Bivocational Clergy Becoming the New Normal? An Analysis of the Current Population Survey, 1996–2017," *Journal for the Scientific Study of Religion* 58(2):523.

6. Pew Research Center, "In U.S., Decline of Christianity Continues at a Rapid Pace: An Update on America's Changing Religious Landscape," Oct. 17, 2019. Report describes Pew's survey results from 2018 and 2019. https://www.pewforum.org /2019/10/17/in-u-s-decline-of-christianity-continues-at-rapid -pace/

7. "American Congregations 2015," 3, 9.

8. *The Ministry in Historical Perspectives*, eds. H. Richard Niebuhr and Daniel D. Williams, (Harper & Brothers, New York: 1956), 49.

9. E. Brooks Holifield, *God's Ambassadors: A History of the Christian Clergy in America* (Grand Rapids: Wm. B. Eerdmans, 2007), 28–29.

10. Holifield, p. 116.

11. Julie Zauzmer, "The circuit preacher was an idea of the frontier past. Now it's the cutting-edge response to shrinking churches," *The Washington Post*, Sept. 23, 2019. https:// www.washingtonpost.com/religion/the-circuit-preacher-was-an -idea-of-the-frontier-past-now-its-the-cutting-edge-response-to -shrinking-churches/2019/09/23/e3cced32-d348-11e9-9343- 40db57cf6abd_story.html

12. 2016 author interview with E. Brooks Holifield.

13. 2016 author interview with E. Brooks Holifield.

CHAPTER 2: SURE, I CAN GIVE A SERMON

1. An analysis by Rick Morse, vice president of Hope Partnership for Missional Transformation, finds a congregation typically needs at least 130 in average Sunday attendance in order to sustainably afford a full-time pastor's compensation package of salary, housing allowance, and benefits. Hope Partnership is an independent consulting ministry with roots in and close ties to the Christian Church (Disciples of Christ).

2. Stephen Ministries is a nonprofit that provides Christ-centered training for laypeople to help others through difficult life transitions. See https://www.stephenministries.org/default.cfm.

CHAPTER 3: FROM LEAD ACTOR
TO BEST SUPPORTING CAST

1. Frank Newport, "Mississippi Retains Standing as Most Religious State," Feb. 8, 2017. The report sums up highlights from Gallup's survey of religiosity by state in 2016, https://news.gallup.com/poll/203747/mississippi-retains-standing-religious-state.aspx.

2. Martha Grace Reese, *Unbinding the Gospel: Real Life Evangelism* (St. Louis, MO: Chalice Press, 2nd ed., 2018).

3. Data comes from author's August 2019 interview with Messy Church USA Executive Director Roberta Egli. For more information on the movement, visit messychurchusa.org.

4. Acton Congregational Church has not switched from full- to part-time. It has had a part-time pastor for decades and for as long as congregants can remember. It's included nonetheless in the author's study because the church has been on a steady path to increased vitality, and its experiences can be instructive for part-time congregations seeking new ways to thrive.

5. "Pastoral Compensation, 2019," New England Conference, The United Methodist Center, Office of Administrative Services, 2. https://www.neumc.org/files/tables/content /8891066/fields/files/7a8422dc832d482aab08c608b3a66102/ pastoral+compensation+2019+dg.pdf.

CHAPTER 4: IS THAT A REAL CHURCH?

1. Frank Newport, "Mississippi Retains Standing as Most Religious State," Feb. 8, 2017, https://news.gallup.com/poll /203747/mississippi-retains-standing-religious-state.aspx.

2. Wallschlaeger attends St. John's. Her husband, Joseph Smith, is the pastor.

3. Well-Being Survey of the United Methodist Church Active Clergy—2017, p. 8. https://www.wespath.org/assets/1/7/5058 .pdf.

4. May 2019 interview with Rae Jean Proeschold-Bell of Duke University's Clergy Health Initiative in which she summarized findings from a 2016 survey.

5 Basic life insurance eligibility rules from the UCC Pension Boards: https://www.pbucc.org/index.php/sep-lidi/basic-life -insurance

6. Canons of the Episcopal Church: Title III, Ministry. Canon 9, Sec. (e)(1) https://episcopalchurch.org/files/attached -files/candc_2012pp67-125_1.pdf

7. "The Parochial Report and the Pension Fund: Deputy Committee Studies How We Measure, What We Pay," by Rebecca Wilson in *House of Deputies News*. March 16, 2016. https://deputynews.org/529-2/

8. "Are Bivocational Clergy Becoming the New Normal? An Analysis of the Current Population Survey, 1996–2017" in *Journal for the Scientific Study of Religion* (2019) 58(2):513–25.

9. Francesca Friday, "More Americans Are Single Than Ever Before—and They're Healthier Too," *Observer*, Jan. 16,

2018. Article cites 2017 Census report on marital status in US population, https://observer.com/2018/01/more-americans-are -single-than-ever-before-and-theyre-healthier-too.

10. Kirk Hadaway and Penny Long Marler, "What Pastors Get Paid and When It's Not Enough," *The Christian Century*, June 6, 2019, https://www.christiancentury.org/article/critical -essay/what-pastors-get-paid-and-when-it-s-not-enough.

11. "Are Bivocational Clergy Becoming the New Normal?" 513–25.

12. Newport, "Mississippi Retains Standing."

13. Information on this model of trades-supported church is found here: https://simplewoo.org/trades/

CHAPTER 5: LEARNING FOR THE MANY

1. 2018 Annual Report of the Association of Theological Schools, https://www.ats.edu/uploads/resources/publications -presentations/colloquy-online/2018-annual-report.pdf, 10.

2. 2018 Annual Report of ATS, 10.

3. 2018 Annual Report of ATS, 10.

4. Details on the program and distinctions among ministry certificates are found here: https://www.maineucc.org/wp -content/uploads/2018/10/Ross-MESOM-Curriculum-V3.4 -Intro-24Oct18.pdf.

5. The Iona School of Ministry 2018–2019 general infor-mational brochure, http://www.ionaschool.com/uploads/7/5/9 /7/75978349/general_informational_brochure_2018-2019.pdf.

6. Association of Theological Schools, 2018–2019 Annual Data Tables, https://www.ats.edu/uploads/resources/ institutional-data/annual-data-tables/2018-2019-annual-data -tables.pdf.

7. ATS Annual Data Tables, 12

8. Asset mapping exercises in the Maine Conference of the UCC often draw on *The Power of Asset Mapping: How Your*

Congregation Can Act on Its Gifts by Luther K. Snow (Herndon, VA: Alban Institute, 2004).

CHAPTER 6: TEAMING UP

1. "Freelancing in America: 2018, report from Freelancers Union," 3, https://assets.freelancersunion.org/media/documents/freelancinginamericareport-2018.pdf.
2. Freelancing in America: 2017, report from Freelancers Union, 2, https://assets.freelancersunion.org/media/documents/FreelancingInAmericaReport-2017.pdf.
3. Freelancing in America: 2018, 4.
4. G. Jeffrey MacDonald, "Wonderfully Made: How Churches Are Seizing on Gallery Spaces for Art," Religion News Service, March 27, 2017, https://religionnews.com/2017/03/27/wonderfully-made-how-churches-are-seizing-on-gallery-spaces-for-art.
5. Søren Kierkegaard, "Purity of Heart," (SV XI 114-15) reprinted in *Parables of Kierkegaard*, Thomas C. Oden, ed. (Princeton University Press, 1978), 180–81.
6. "Factors Linked with Religious Knowledge," Pew Research Center, Sept. 28, 2010, https://www.pewforum.org/2010/09/28/u-s-religious-knowledge-survey-factors-linked-with-religious-knowledge.
7. G. Jeffrey MacDonald, "Old Hymns, Fresh Grooves," *The Living Church*, October 9, 2019.
8. G. Jeffrey MacDonald, "Young Singers Revive Parish," *The Living Church*, April 29, 2016, https://livingchurch.org/2016/04/29/young-singers-revive-parish.

CPSIA information can be obtained
at www.ICGtesting.com
Printed in the USA
LVHW050152250221
679870LV00004B/104

9 780664 265991